Precious in Her Father's Eyes

List of Contributors

Edna Doll wrote Carla's eulogy, as well as the following chapters. She also contributed several of the photos in this book.

Chapter 16	The G-Tube Caper
Epilogue	The Beginning—Memories

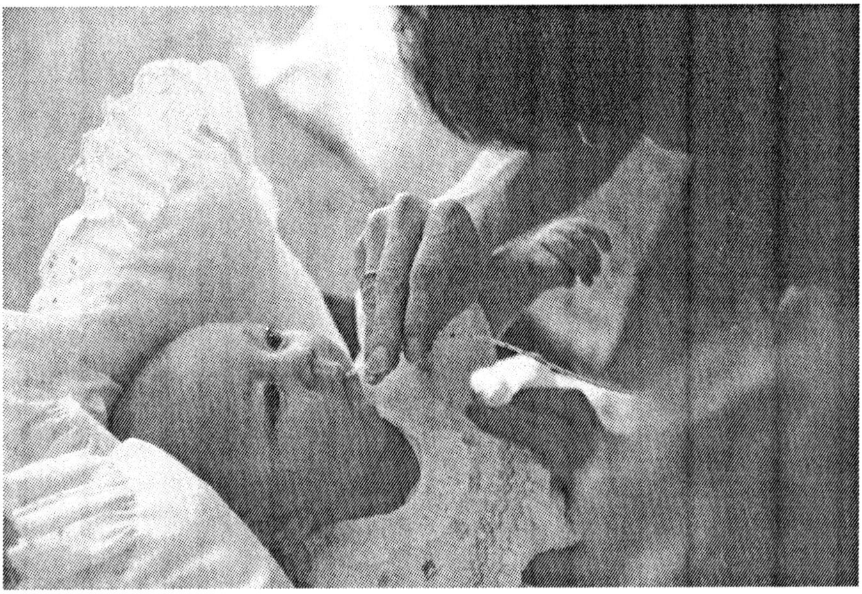

Carla Marie Snyder
1992–1995

Precious in Her Father's Eyes

Carla Marie Snyder 1992–1995

Cynthia Snyder, D. C.

Writers Club Press
San Jose New York Lincoln Shanghai

Precious in Her Father's Eyes
Carla Marie Snyder 1992–1995

Writers Club Press
an imprint of iUniverse.com, Inc.

For information address:
iUniverse.com, Inc.
5220 S 16th, Ste. 200
Lincoln, NE 68512
www.iuniverse.com

Cover design by Julia Wargaski

ISBN: 0-595-12763-0

Printed in the United States of America

Dedication

To Carla,
and to all special children everywhere
and the people who love them.

Epigraph

Count it all joy, my brethren, when you meet various trials, for you know that the testing of your faith produces steadfastness.

James 1:2
Revised Standard Version

But I offer all I am

for the mercy of your plan…

Lighten my darkness,

pour over me your holiness…

Help me be strong

Breath of Heaven (Mary's Song)

Amy Grant

Table of Contents

Preface

CARLA
1992–1995
A EULOGY
GIVEN AT CARLA'S FUNERAL

Carla died on April 5, 1995 at the age of two.
Her eulogy was written by Edna Doll, her great aunt,
and read by her uncle, Carl Dale.

One might say that for the last two years our family has been on a journey to a foreign land. We spoke a different language with words like nebulizer, monitor, tracheotomy. We practiced different rituals: banging sticks together, rattling stones in a can, flashing black pictures on a screen. We lived in a different time zone governed by patterning, feeding schedules and walks to the dark room. Our journey was one of all-powering love for our darling baby Carla. Our litany of prayers rose over her. Please God, show us the ways to help her, comfort her, take away her pain.

Now He has done that, and suddenly the world is vastly different. We say, "Thy will be done." Our faith is strong. We are grateful our baby need suffer no more. Yet we feel a grievous loss. We pray now for strength to find new paths—to help one another while we carry poignant memories of our precious baby.

In spite of everything, Carla was indeed a fortunate baby, knowing only love for her whole existence. She had the unstinting and magnificent care of Cindy and Bob, and Anora too. Anora's caring was almost mind-boggling. Last week as we were taking a walk, Anora stooped to pick up some wild grasses for Carla to smell. Anora knew we were doing sensory activities and thought the wild grasses would help.

There are no words to explain the love and care Cindy and Bob lavished on their baby. Nothing was too much, too big, too small. Nothing was ever overlooked. In the true sense, they gave their very lives to Carla day after day, night after night, week after week. How many nights did they spend on the floor near Carla, ever wakeful of her breathing? To be with them, to see their constant concern, their gentleness and strength in handling Carla was truly inspirational. They did it all with love and grace, never overlooking the needs of Anora.

In some homes faced with so difficult a situation there might have been gloom and doom. Not so at Cindy and Bob's. In spite of weariness and tiredness that cut to the bone, negatives were unknown; "can't" a word unused. Theirs was a home of love and laughter, a celebration of life itself, of Anora and Carla and the goodness of God. There were Christmas and Easter, birthday balloons, big signs, flowers, and innumerable cups of tea for everyone who came in the door. Theirs was a triumph over darkness, a celebration of light and spirit.

Today we celebrate the life of our sweet baby, Carla Marie. In the scale of the universe, her eighteen pounds would seem insignificant. But for those of us who loved her so deeply, she was the most impressive, beautiful, heart-filling baby in the whole world.

True, all babies are special. But Carla was special in so many ways. She was so tiny, but she fought a valiant fight, teaching us lessons we might never have known…lessons in the preciousness of life, in strength over adversity, in caring for each other, awareness and depth of love. She filled our lives, our thoughts, our prayers. It was a privilege to help take care of Carla, to hold her dear small self in our arms. I always felt that privilege and I'm sure her Grandma Claire did too.

It is no accident that Carla came to us at Christmastime, and God has taken her at Easter. Surely here is a message. The message is clear. Carla is not gone. She has only gone ahead. Emily Dickinson, in writing about

Heaven said she was as sure of the place as if a chart were given. Our faith too, is in that direction. I personally promised Carla that whoever got there first, she or I, when we finally met I would hold her close, and we would rock from one end of the Milky Way to the other.

Cindy said Carla is with God in Heaven. Bob said he was sure Carla was in a better place. Anora said Carla is with the angels. They are all right. And there we must leave her in peace and in the comfort she never knew here. We leave her only till we meet again. And here on Earth, Carla will always be with us. Her tiny delicate hands hold our hearts forever.

* * *

This is a story of perseverance, of overcoming huge obstacles, of staying positive when there was every logical reason not to be. It is a story of finding out how much strength truly lies within. Most importantly, it is the story of discovering the gift of selfless love, which truly demands nothing back. This kind of love asks you to give one hundred percent of yourself simply because that is all that you can do, all that you want to do. You have no choice when you love another human being that much.

I want to share this story with you because it could be your story. As a woman, I found out what it really means to be a mother. I learned the rewards of self-sacrifice in a world that sees self-sacrifice as wrong. We are told we should take care of ourselves first.

My story is that of a woman who had it "all" only to find out there was even more to be gained. I look back at my life before Carla and see it as a typical "fluff" existence without substance. As painful as the two years with Carla were, and as painful as the past few have been, I am glad that I have moved beyond that shallow self.

This is a story of many hearts being opened to love all because of one little person who could not smile, laugh, make baby noises, or even look directly at you, to win you over. Without being able to do all these, how did she touch so many lives? How did she manage to make so many people fall in love with her? I, for one, am eternally grateful for what she had to teach because my life will never be the same.

Acknowledgements

Writing this book has been a tremendous challenge—a challenge I could not have faced without the help and support of so many. Thank you to my husband, Bob, and my daughter, Anora for their patience and ongoing love; my friends Barbara Smyly, Carol Kotopoulis, and Jan Kirlew for continued encouragement. My deep appreciation to Edna for contributing to this book with her photographs and two of the chapters. I would also like to thank Joe Cohn, M.D., for his medical expertise in reviewing the book, Joseph V. Jacus for meticulously scanning every photo, and my stepdaughter, Lisa Snyder, for answering my endless computer questions. Rich praise goes to Julia Wargaski for her beautiful, intelligent cover design and enlightened guiding principles.

I am deeply grateful to Anna Jacus for two things: her writing and editing expertise as well as her shared vision of bringing this book to fruition. Without her contribution, this book would have remained only a dream.

And most of all, I thank God for the precious gift of Carla Marie.

Introduction

The Dream...

I woke up in the early hours of the morning with my heart pounding and my hands clenched at my sides, overwhelmed by the sense of foreboding in the dream. "I'll have to call Debbie in the morning and tell her that her daughter may be in danger...'Be careful!'"

The dream was not specific, but a terrible sense of danger permeated its scenes. I could see my girlfriend, Debbie, and her one-year-old daughter. They were playing, laughing, having a good time. And then drastically, it all changed. There was something seriously wrong with her daughter. There was terror on Debbie's face, and she was rushing the baby off somewhere—the dream ended as abruptly as it started.

When I fully awoke in the morning I remembered the dream. But I decided not to call my friend. Why scare her? After all, I was due to give birth any day now. Maybe it was just one of those crazy pregnancy dreams.... Never for a moment did I think the dream had anything to do with me.

Chapter 1

The Foreign Land

My labor was progressing normally that December day, two days before Christmas, and I was more than ready to bring my second child into the world.

It was early in the afternoon when I recognized the sensations of early labor. I had just come home after indulging in chocolate cheesecake and tea with my friend, Jan, when I realized the unmistakable early pains. I groaned to myself, "Oh no. Why did I eat all that rich cake?" I knew I would suffer the consequences later.

My husband, Bob, was nearby as I prepared myself for the labor ahead of me. He took over the care of our four-year-old daughter, Anora. I was attended by a bevy of women. Carol was my friend and personal support. She had arrived for this occasion wearing her usual bright fuchsia lipstick and the beautiful smile that softens her face incredibly. Carol knew how to *be* with people by giving them her full attention. Her presence was a great consolation.

Sophie, my nurse-midwife, would facilitate the delivery with Anna, her assistant. Sophie was a very capable Irish woman who exuded tremendous strength and compassion. There was a no-nonsense air about her. She and Anna both had extensive experience and genuine commitment to their respective roles. Everything was safe, secure, and comfortable in my own bedroom at home. It was unlike my first birth, when I was so inexperienced and fearful.

Sophie was not the same midwife I used last time, but I had quickly become comfortable with her and confident of her abilities. Labor was progressing more smoothly and quickly this time. The only distinct difference was that I knew this baby was much bigger than my last five-and-a-half-pounder because I could feel her so much more as she moved down the birth canal.

At first, Anora seemed quite interested in all the activity of birth. But around ten o'clock she got tired of the whole birthing thing and thankfully went to bed.

Sophie encouraged me to stay with it. She looked me square in the eye while I sat in a rocking chair, moaning. Kneeling at my feet, she held my hand and brushed back loose tendrils of hair.

It was only an hour after midnight when I was in the final stages of birth. My committed friend, Carol, anchored me to the bedroom wall against the labor pains. I could feel tremendous pressure as my baby came down the birth canal. I heard Carol's enthusiastic encouragement, "You're doing a great job honey. Soon you are going to see your baby!"

She was also talking to the baby with the same enthusiasm, "We're looking forward to seeing you soon, baby. You are very welcome here." It was a thrill for her to be part of a new life emerging.

I was most aware of how profusely I was sweating. My nightgown was stuck to my body. My hair was plastered to my forehead. I could feel the red flush in my cheeks. I was very aware of how hard I was working physically, and at the same time I was having the thought, "I must be crushing Carol against the wall by leaning so heavily against her." She had her arms securely under my armpits as I half-stood and half-leaned against her. Sophie reached her hands between my legs and felt the head of my baby. "Here—let me get a mirror so you can see your baby's head." She and Carol tried to get me to share the enthusiasm of this glimpse. I took a peek at the head barely visible in the mirror…

The elation of the moment turned to agony with the next powerful contraction. My knees weakened with all the incredible pressure. I went down on all fours, grabbing onto the side of the bed with my arms. All of a sudden, Sophie's voice took on an entirely different tone.

"You need to push this baby out as quickly as possible. Push as hard as you can," she commanded. Sensing the urgency in her voice, I pushed with all my might. Out came a baby girl, and immediately, out came my placenta which had separated in utero.

The baby was blue from lack of oxygen. She was not breathing, and she was not moving. Sophie and Anna furiously began delivering CPR to her. The two minutes crept into an eternity...Finally, I heard Sophie say, "I have a heartbeat." And my husband ran off to call 9-1-1.

Everything had a surreal feel to it. I was acutely aware of the intense feeling in the room. There was no sense of panic, just an intensity. I don't think my mind was perceiving what was going on—that at any moment my baby could die.

As this was going on, I was lying on the floor unable to move, and in such incredible pain. All I could manage to do was turn my head and reach my hand out towards my baby. The only sound was the conversation between Sophie and Anna. There was no anticipated cry.

It seemed that only moments later the rescue squad was there. Three more people crowded around my baby on the floor. The tone in the room changed to business-like activity. They were inserting a tube down her throat to deliver oxygen into her lungs and preparing to take her to our local hospital. Through all they were doing, she made no noise whatsoever.

For some reason there was also a police officer standing in the corner, looking on. I remember sensing his awkwardness at seeing my sprawled, half-naked body in a bloody mess on my bedroom floor. He shifted his weight, averted his eyes, and tried to look busy.

In an instant, they were taking my baby away. Sophie was going in the ambulance with her, and I was glad for that because I knew Sophie would be strong and encouraging for her. As they were about to leave, Sophie turned to me and asked, "Cindy, what is your baby's name?" I could see it was important for her to know.

"Carla," I breathed. "Carla is her name." I would find out later that Carla means strong. Strong is what she proved to be during the next two years of frequent health crises and innumerable hospitalizations. I added Marie as her middle name. Marie means blessed. Later I would come to see how blessed she was—for she had the strongest love possible from family and friends.

Another ambulance came for me after about ten minutes. In a few minutes, my husband and I were on our way to the hospital as well. Carol would stay at the house with Anora, who thankfully had slept through the whole commotion. I was leaving my one baby in the safety and warmth of my house so that I could follow the other into the world of emergency and fear.

Before I was wheeled away I said to my friend, "Carol, please call my friend Jan. Ask her to start a prayer chain for Carla." I knew Jan would not mind being awakened at 2 A.M. for such a reason. It was the first of many prayers to be answered by many people for Carla.

At the hospital, they gave me intravenous magnesium sulfate to get my skyrocketing blood pressure back down to normal. By now it had gone up to 212/110. My reflexes were also brisk. They diagnosed me with preeclampsia of sudden onset, with placental abruption.

As the nurses bustled around my room taking care of me, my husband, Bob, was standing alone in the hallway outside. I heard Sophie come over to be with him and I could hear them talking quietly. I heard him saying how hard it was to see a baby start off like this and I heard him break down in those words and start to cry. I could sense his body momentarily crumbling; his broad, strong shoulders falling down. My rock of a husband was allowing himself to feel the grief and sorrow of what was happening to our child. I could hear the murmur of Sophie's comforting words. I was so grateful she was there.

What seemed like an eternity later they wheeled me into the room where Carla was being carefully watched. The pediatrician on call that night was a tall, imposing man with sandy hair and glasses. He spoke unemotionally, explaining that the tube into Carla's trachea had to be reinserted, that the intensive care unit at Jefferson Wood Hospital had been notified, and that she would be transferred later in the day.

The peculiar way the doctor spoke worried me. I wondered why he was being so aloof and robotic. Was he judging us for having had a home birth? I felt I was in a precarious position and wondered what was happening to Sophie. Whatever it was, I knew she could handle it with her calm and professional demeanor. She knew as well as they did, that this freak occurrence could have happened just as easily in their hospital setting. There had been nothing in my pregnancy to indicate such an outcome.

I reached out to touch Carla's hand. It was totally limp, but so very warm. The warmth connected me to her aliveness. "I love you, honey. I'm right here with you and so is your dad," I murmured to her encouragingly. She was lying naked under the most intense bright light. I could see her closed eyes tearing from the intensity of it, but I was afraid to ask if anything could be done about it. She was clearly in this doctor's control.

It was surreal—so hard to comprehend—that an anticipated home birth would end up in this room, in this hospital, in such a crisis. I was supposed to be lying at home with my new daughter swaddled in my arms. This was to have been our time of joy. Anora would have been awakened to share her baby sister's first moments with us. We were supposed to be blissfully happy right now, whispering quietly at the joy of her perfect little body, counting toes and fingers. It was not to be. We never could have imagined what lay ahead for us.

That morning was extremely tough. Hours later, the staff finally said they would bring Carla in for me to say good-by before taking her to the other hospital. They rolled her in. Members of the neonatal care unit followed her cart. This was a somber looking group. Expressionless, and all business. They did not introduce themselves or address me by name.

It was such a contrast, I couldn't help being startled. I was all emotion, and they were all routine. They had been through this hundreds of times. For me, it was utterly new and foreign.

That moment was a flurry of activity. A pile of papers was being pushed at me to sign. The male nurse described the procedures represented by each consent form in a monotone. "And this next one we need you to sign is a consent for a spinal tap."

"What!" I exclaimed, taken aback as my mind raced for a reason why they would want to do a spinal tap. I knew how painful spinal taps were, and I knew Carla showed none of the medical symptoms necessitating one. "I can't see why you would need to do that. No. I don't consent to that test," I replied.

Without looking up or losing a moment, he proceeded again to speak about signing this paper. Again I refused. "No. There is no reason to do that." As if he never heard me, he proceeded to roll right along with his protocol. This time the nurse who had been taking care of me chimed in. Like an angel she rescued me from the futility of this scene.

"Excuse me," she said. "I think the mother is trying to tell you she is not going to authorize you to do a spinal tap." I looked up at her, somewhat surprised. I thanked God that someone was listening to me. She clearly understood my feelings. I'm sure she also knew I had little strength for verbal combat right now. With that, he actually looked up at us, received the communication, and stopped the barrage.

Finally they were done, and Carla and I were left alone in the room together. I looked down at my daughter lying there with a tube down her throat, intravenous lines in her arms and legs, electrodes with wiring all over her chest. She was so still, her eyes closed.

"I love you, Carla," was all I could manage to say. Then they came and whisked her away. I was all alone in the room. So very, very alone.

My friend, Carol, and my midwife, Sophie, supporting me during labor

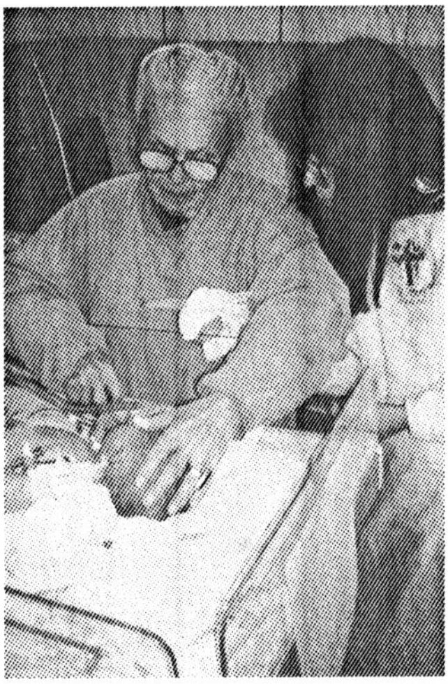

Edna Doll, Cindy's aunt, and Lisa Snyder, Cindy's stepdaughter, at Carla's bedside in the first week

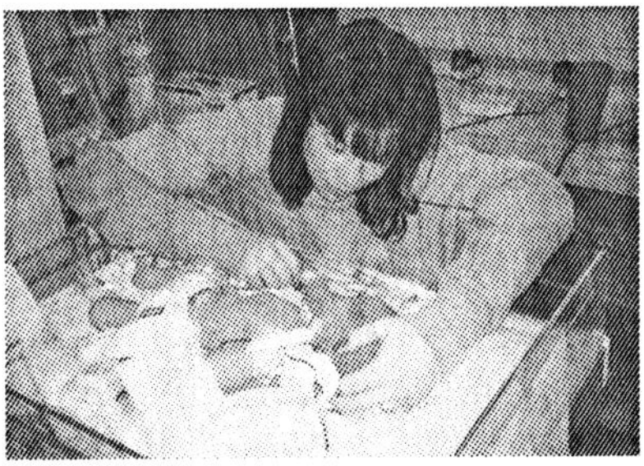

Cindy Snyder with Carla in the neonatal care unit during the first week, when Carla was still on life support

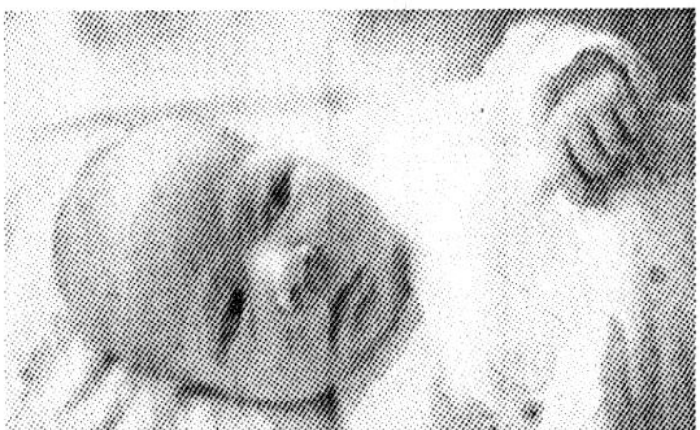

Carla, still in the neonatal intensive care unit, at six weeks old. She was detached from all breathing equipment for the first time, and doing fine on her own.

Carla sleeping peacefully with her pink ribbon, so everyone will know it's a girl!

Chapter 2

Loving Presence

"Edna, please go to Jefferson Wood Hospital as soon as possible. Find Carla. Tell the staff her mother said you are to be by her side as much as possible."

I knew someone from our family had to be at the hospital so that Carla would know our presence and love; so she would not be alone. I knew my Aunt Edna would be the perfect person to do this.

Edna was small, about 5'2", but of solid build. Her white hair had been worn parted in the middle, then pulled up into a French braid for thirty-plus years. She was my father's sister, and she'd been intimately involved in my life since I was an infant. She never married or had children of her own. My brother and I became her children and I was very close to her. Edna had been a teacher and school principal for many years. Her joyful spirit and her connection to children were unique. I trusted her to deliver my love to my daughter.

"This is what I want you to say to Carla.... Tell her I cannot be with her because they will not release me for twenty-four hours. Tell her how much her mommy and daddy love her. Tell her how strong she is and how much we want her to live." I could feel how intensely she was listening to my every word, how much she wanted to get this right, how much it meant to me. I stopped abruptly with the string of words. I knew it didn't matter that she repeat me word for word. The love and caring that would pour out of her for Carla would make all the difference. All I really wanted Carla to know was that she was loved, and not abandoned. I knew that love needed to be present as she was undergoing painful testing and procedures by medical staff who were in the business of attending to the physical body. I wanted Carla's emotional and spiritual body to receive attention as well. In my heart I knew that was just as important for her survival.

After sending Edna to deliver all the love and support I could offer I was exhausted. It was now getting late in the evening...Christmas Eve already. Right now, the rest of the world was busy with last minute Christmas preparations. Children were excitedly awaiting Santa's visit. Families were heading off to church. And here I was—alone in a hospital bed.

But the absence of a Currier and Ives postcard scene was barely a flicker in my mind. So much had happened since we had arrived in the early morning hour that it seemed I had been here for days already. I was in such a state of physical pain and emotional turmoil that I couldn't even guess what time of day it was. My nurse suggested I try to get some sleep. What a comical idea! Sleep, during this most horrendous time of my life? It seemed impossible, but I finally drifted off.

I woke up in the early morning, temporarily disoriented. I expected to see the familiar decor of my bedroom. Instead, my eyes found the walls of a maternity room. I didn't hear Anora's laugher. I heard the tones and repeated announcements from the hospital corridor. And then it hit me so hard: I was all alone in a hospital without my little girl. I had no idea what was happening to her in a strange hospital. Who was with her? Who was touching her and holding her little hand? Was she in pain? Was she awake? I wasn't there to see. I wasn't there to be with her. Both of us were alone in places I never dreamed we would be in; places I strongly felt should be avoided.

The phone rang. It was my friend, Carol, who had been with me when Carla was born. This was the first time I was hearing her voice since those chaotic early moments of Carla's life. "Good morning," she said cheerfully,

"It's Christmas Day. I always like to do something for someone on this day. Would you like it if I came over and rebirthed you?"

"Sure Carol. That sounds great. I just don't know how much uninterrupted time we will have in this hospital room with nurses coming in and out all the time," I replied.

"Oh, we'll just put up a 'do not disturb' sign on the door," she said light-heartedly.

I knew this would be a good thing for me to do at this point. I had been doing this type of deep, connected breathing called rebirthing for some time. It helped release a lot of old trauma and upsets from my past. After several of these sessions I had felt so peaceful and connected to God. They were truly blissful experiences that put me in a place of comfort. I could use some of that now for sure.

Soon Carol was at my bedside. Just seeing her familiar face was a comfort. While she leaned her tall angular body back into her chair, I immediately settled back in my bed as comfortably as I could, and with her guidance, I started the breathing. I gave it my all. I was breathing for myself and for Carla, for all the upset of not knowing what was to be. I was concentrating so hard on breathing and exhaling deeply and fully that I lost my sense of time and space for awhile. I filled myself up with new air, taking in through my lungs the energy I needed to get strong again. The breathing helped with the physical pain and soon I came to the point of deep and total relaxation.

Suddenly I knew I was done with the deep breathing. I felt a surge of renewed energy and also something else. I sensed the presence and peace of God in that room with us, and I felt rather than heard the words, "Everything is going to be alright." I opened my eyes to look at Carol, wondering if she had sensed this peaceful presence as well.

"Everything is going to be alright, Carol," I said with calmness.

"I felt a loving warmth in this room," she said with a peaceful smile. We just looked at each other. There was nothing else to say. We had been uninterrupted for a good half an hour. I'm sure that was no coincidence.

For the first time since the traumatic birth I felt relaxed and calm. A new nurse started her shift. She was sincerely distressed over my situation and talked on and on about how awful all this was, shaking her head all the while. "And for such a thing to happen at Christmas. Oh my." She just couldn't stop herself from continuing with how dreadful all this was. I had the image of a distressed chicken running around in circles, clucking loudly.

This is not what I wanted to hear. I had no desire to share my extraordinary experience and my certainty that everything was going to be okay. But in my mind I said, "Be still woman. Don't you know who my daughter is? She is strong and she will be alright." I was certain of it.

Several hours later I was gratefully released from the hospital. At home, some family members awaited me, and lots of beautifully wrapped packages. It was a festive looking scene although the strain showed on my family's faces. My mother was crying and praying to my departed father for help from heaven. My brother asked a lot of concerned questions about Carla. It was hard to be in their pain and upset when I had so much of my own to deal with. Mostly I was just very tired. All I wanted was to be with Carla.

"All I really want to do is take a shower and go to the hospital and see my baby," I told everyone. "I hope you understand I just can't do presents right now." As quickly as I could, I went to the shower. The warm water felt so cleansing on my body. It was as if I was washing away the fear and pain of the day. The water was like a baptism, renewing and replenishing my spirit. I was ready to go on.

In a short time my brother was driving me down the highway to see Carla. I tried to imagine seeing her in this place. What would it be like? My mind created a vision of masked nurses and doctors and dismal looking rooms. I saw myself turning a corner. I was scared and excited all at once.

At the hospital we found a wheelchair for me. I was too weak to walk very far. My brother and I made jokes about not banging me into any walls on the way up to see Carla. Although I joked and kidded around, my heart was pounding like crazy on the inside. The guard let us onto the elevator that would go upstairs to the NICU, the Neonatal Intensive Care Unit.

It was like entering an alien land. The intensive care unit was one huge room full of babies lying side by side in little plastic isolettes. Bright lights on machines were blinking and loud threatening noises blared from them. It was an environment of complete sensory overload. I couldn't believe how loud it was. Didn't all that noise wake up or upset the babies? Why weren't the nurses responding to the beeps and blares of the monitors? Did all that noise mean everything was going well?

The babies were obviously accustomed to all that noise. They weren't crying or screaming. I walked down the line of these fragile children and realized from their size that they were either premature or too very, very sick to protest. Of course, the nurses were able to distinguish between the alarms that meant danger, and the routine noise.

At the end of the line of babies was Carla. She was hooked up to several machines with intravenous lines and attachments extending in every direction. The tears came up so hard and swift as I realized this is how she was starting her life. I hardly knew where to touch her. I stroked her head. I held her small beautiful hands. "Mommy is here, sweetheart. Your mom is right here with you now." I was so happy to see her, so overwhelmed to finally be with my child again. She was so beautiful—electrodes, intravenous lines and all. I just felt so grateful that she was alive.

The doctor in charge held himself stiffly and spoke in short, cryptic sentences. His dark eyes looked off somewhere over our heads. He had nothing encouraging to say and he said it all in the most discouraging way. He described her severe loss of oxygen at birth, her abnormal blood tests…. She was on medication to control her blood pressure, and many additional tests would be performed. So many things were wrong I could hardly take it all in. This doctor exuded his medical authority over us. He invited no questions, looked for no participation. It seemed all he could imagine doing was delivering bad news.

Chapter 3

A Family Vigil

My family formed a vigil over Carla, each of us taking different shifts at her bedside. We all had our different ways of being with her. My mother had the morning shift. In her quiet way, she would sit next to Carla, always dressed immaculately, telling her granddaughter gently how much she loved her, and buying soft baby things to put in her crib.

I stayed with Carla from lunch until dinnertime, when my husband arrived. My husband, Bob, tall, strong, and handsome, was all soft and sweet with his baby. He touched her gently with his strong hands, reassuring her that Daddy was here looking on her with obvious love in his pale blue eyes.

The final shift, late at night, was all Edna's. Our vigils made it possible for someone who loved Carla to be with her from nine in the morning until eleven at night; sometimes even later, when Edna just couldn't leave her.

In her blue jeans and sneakers, my aunt, Edna, would talk and sing endlessly to Carla. Working her way subtly into everyone's heart, she could easily determine who was good for Carla and who was not. She learned the story of all who worked there because everyone warmed to her.

The first formal confrontation with the "powers that be" in the hospital happened after only several days in the intensive care unit. I hadn't given it a thought. To me everything was going smoothly. I had no reason to believe we were violating any rule in the ICU. I had noticed a sign stating visitors were limited to immediate family, and I had just lumped all of us in that category. But our visitations did not go unnoticed by the head nurse—the one who ruled. This nurse was the smallest in the unit, but clearly, she was in charge. Her entire demeanor exuded authority.

She arrived with a social worker one afternoon and asked, "Mrs. Snyder, could you come with us for a few moments please?" I thought they were going to prepare me for whatever had to happen to Carla next. I had no idea of what was to come. They sat me down in a chair, one stood in front of me and one stood to the side, both towering above me. "We brought you in here to tell you that you have been violating the visitors policy. We have noticed that your family is here all the time. That is not fair to other grandparents who are not allowed here in the 'off' hours. So we want to inform you that your family will not be allowed either."

The social worker turned her head towards me and with a sweet, condescending voice added her agreement, "The rules in the ICU are for everyone, you know."

With a sinking, sickening feeling I realized what was going on. It was an attempt to intimidate a parent and enforce a rule that offered no sense or empathy for the well-being of a baby. However, I was not the typical easily-intimidated-by-medical-superiority parent, and this would be their first opportunity to find that out. I realized the bull of their argument. Even after a few days, we had all noticed that very often we were the only ones present with our baby in that room. Many babies barely had visitors, and some had none.

"No, I don't think you understand how we do things in my family," I said in a shaky but strong voice. "It is so important for Carla to be surrounded by family love at this critical point in her life. This is a crisis and we do for each other what needs to be done." I anticipated their next argument.

"You know we always get out of the nurses' way when they need to do their work. We have caused no interference and no unfairness to other parents whatsoever." I tried to continue but my strength was leaving me. I couldn't say more. I lost it. I just started to cry. They had gotten to me—a mother physically and emotionally drained. I don't remember what was said next but we ended up agreeing that only grandparents would be permitted. I wasn't about to say, "And what about aunts?" at that point. Our secret as to whose parent Edna was would be a source of confusion and mystery to the nursing staff and a source of comic relief for us. We would need these occasional light moments for all the upcoming trials in the weeks ahead of us in the ICU. If lying about Edna's identity brought us some relief, then so be it. Edna was going to stay. Carla needed her and we needed her. No hospital rule was going to take her away from us.

Chapter 4

Denying Our Limits

"Carla has a case of pneumonia. Her X-rays show infiltrates in the right lobe. This is all connected to the asphyxia at birth and her inability to swallow. Too many secretions have made their way into her lungs." With this news reverberating in our brains we walked out of the ICU and sat down. We were shocked and devastated. We asked ourselves how a baby so young, and in such a fragile condition could survive pneumonia...

A pretty blonde nurse who had been taking care of Carla came by and saw the looks on our faces. "Your baby is strong, you know," she said with an air of confidence, "She can pull through this." The tone of her voice changed our attitudes in a moment. My mind switched from, "She is going to die," to "Maybe—yes. She can get through this!" This nurse was the first of many earthly angels God would put in our path for reassurance. We got ourselves up and went back to Carla's side. Later we would find out how common pneumonia was in the ICU and that most babies survived. But we were new to this. We had no clue.

As the days went by I learned firsthand all the things that her little body could not do. Every system had been seriously affected because the control center, her brain, had been so badly injured. Not just her physical movements, but her breathing, digestion, elimination, swallowing, even something as simple as a gag reflex was missing. All of the functions that we expect to work automatically could not function in Carla's body...She'd been deprived of oxygen for too long.

I was also learning to become quite a detective. I checked up on what was done to Carla and how often. I figured out which nurses were great and which ones were mediocre. There were several advantages to the ICU setup. The obvious one was that it was easier for the nurses to get to a baby quickly. The second was that I had the chance to listen to a lot of their important conversations. One morning I overheard one nurse commenting to another. She was concerned because it seemed the babies' heels had to be pricked much more frequently in this hospital than in the last one she had worked in. That made my antennae go up because I wanted to ensure that Carla would not be overtested or subjected to unnecessary painful procedures. I also realized that since Carla had been stabilized, many of these blood tests probably did not have to be done so often. At this point, her heels, like those of all the other babies, had so many needle pricks I don't know how they ever found new places to prick. I immediately went to the neonatologist and asked for longer intervals. He agreed without a hassle. It was just another one of those routine procedures.

This group of neonatologists, who were probably used to every procedure and test going unquestioned by parents, were probably in a state of disarray with me because I was no typical parent. I had enough experience in the medical field before I became a chiropractor to know medical doctors were not always right. I'm sure they thought I was just one to "make waves", but if they only knew how difficult it was for me to constantly challenge, question, and speak up, they would have been surprised. I was unwilling for Carla's experience to be any more unpleasant than it had to be. That's why I was willing to take on any nurse or doctor that treated my daughter without consideration.

One morning I saw the pediatric neurologist examining Carla. As he didn't see me I thought I would just stay back and watch what he was going to do. He did all the familiar testing of the reflexes, but there was something wrong with the picture. As I watched him examine Carla I knew in an instant why I had disliked him the other day. It was like watching a butcher examine a piece of meat—the careless way he touched and moved her, the brevity of it. His total detachment belied the fact that he was touching a human being. I could feel my anger rising. He looked up; our eyes met. I had to walk over and let him know how I felt.

"I really do not like how you handle my daughter," I said directly to his face. "And I do not think that I want you to be examining her anymore in the future at all." He looked at me—shocked.

"Well, she needs to be examined while she is here."

"Well, I will see who else can come, but I am quite certain it will not be you." He looked at me with fury and walked away.

After taking a few deep breaths, I found the head neonatologist on duty that day and explained my feelings. First of all, why did Carla need to be checked by a neurologist daily when her neurological status was quite apparent and she had been thoroughly analyzed by her current doctors? He agreed the neurologist did not need to come so often. It was just the referral setup of the hospital—the way everybody's hands get in the till.

I thanked God for my medical background! It was coming in handy now. I was clearly at an advantage, having been a medical lab technician, and having worked in doctor's offices and hospitals. Also, in chiropractic school we took many medical courses. I only wished I had more information in this area of intensive care. There was too much I was unfamiliar with.

The sweetest doctors were the residents. They had not been around long enough to develop the tough protective shell and the authoritative manner. They always tried to answer my questions and made me feel human and equal. I wondered how long that would last. I prayed they would remain as they were now—kind and competent in equal measures. One of them had saved Carla's life. It all happened so quickly. But that's how it was with Carla; she was fine one moment and in danger the next.

I was right at her bedside when her color started turning bluish-grey. I yelled for a nearby nurse. She came over and yelled for the resident who was also nearby. I moved away from the bed and prayed for Carla, "Please be okay." As quickly as it happened, it was over. She was breathing again. She had experienced another incident of reflux, where food comes up from the stomach. Unfortunately, since she could not swallow, she was literally choking. The resident gave orders to keep her in a more upright position.

One morning as I entered the ICU, I was surprised to see a familiar face standing at Carla's bedside. It was Dr. Kane, a family doctor I had met several times at the home births of my patients. He was the rare doctor, willing to come to a patient's home to examine a baby. I did home visits for my patients as well, so we had the chance to meet. Through the grapevine he had learned of Carla's predicament.

There was something so completely different in the way he touched Carla during his exam. Even the way he stood there looking at Carla with compassion warmed my heart. "Dr. Kane," I said with relief, "How nice to see you here." I was moved by his offer of sympathy over Carla's condition and relieved to speak to a medical doctor whose empathy lightened my worries.

"Please give me your opinion of what has happened to Carla."

"Well, a lot of what initially happened is typical when the body experiences such a crisis of oxygen deprivation." He spoke at length of the typical bodily reactions: reduced urine output, lowered blood pressure; many functions are lowered in an attempt to preserve the life of the body. In other words many of the things that happened to Carla in the first forty-eight hours were all "normal" reactions considering what she had been through. It all made so much sense to me as he spoke, and it reminded me of the infinite wisdom of the body. The body always knows what to do and does the best it can under every circumstance. But why hadn't the other doctors explained it to us this way? All we were told was that everything was abnormal.

"Thank you so much for the information," I said with great relief. "Right now my big concerns are her lethargy and weak reflexes. Everyone keeps telling us she is just not coming around."

"Well, yes she could be somewhat lethargic," Dr. Kane explained. "She is on a high dose of phenobarbitol, which is a brain suppressant."

Click! went my brain. Of course. She was on such a high dose that, in essence, she was doped up. Who could have a normal neurological check-up in that condition? I knew instinctively she did not need to be on this high dose anymore. The only seizure she ever had was an arm twitch on the ambulance ride over to this hospital. They had kept her on the same dose since that time. I knew she needed to be weaned off this drug. I knew again it was just another one of those routine procedures done on babies like Carla.

The last bit of information he offered was for me, personally. He knew I was agitated about the phenobarbitol and was going to demand she be tapered off it. He looked at me intently and ran his hands quickly through his unruly hair. "Now, when you speak to the neonatologist, remember, they do not like to be told what to do. Rather, ask them what can be done about the dosage instead of demanding withdrawal."

How did he know I could be totally tactless, almost militant in my demands when it came to Carla? It was his subtle way of telling me not to rock the boat—too hard. I did know I had to keep my cool in this hospital environment. I knew parents who had their children taken away from them because they spoke up too many times in opposition to medical directives. I knew the power of the medical system. They had the power to take a child from your custody if you did not agree to all their ways. I also felt that despite the fact that my outspokenness was a thorn in their side, they knew how devoted I was to my child. Anyone could see how devoted my whole family was to Carla—we wanted the best for her. My commitment to my daughter was greater than my fear of their power.

"You know, you look very pale. You need to take care of yourself too," Dr. Kane remarked gently to me. I hadn't really looked at myself too much in the past week. I knew I wasn't physically strong yet. It was still an effort to walk and stand up for any length of time. But I had no major concern for myself. Every bit of energy I had was for Carla. She was the one who needed strength right now. She was the one who had to keep knowing how much I loved her, how much we wanted her to be here with us. So even if I was pale and anemic I was going to be there for my baby. Nothing could keep me away.

Lucky for me, it was the beginning of January now and a new neonatologist was on duty for the month. Dr. Rack was a short, handsome man with a kind and concerned air about him. "Dr. Rack," I said, pulling him aside to have a private conversation. "I would like to have a conversation with you about changing the dosage of phenobarbitol Carla is on. I don't understand how she can be expected to have any normal reactions when she is on such a high dose. Also, I haven't seen any notes of seizure episodes since the time her arm twitched on the ambulance ride over here."

Instantly I could see him stiffen up. His whole attitude towards me changed. "Well, that is not recommended at this point in time," he stated flatly. Like a game of badminton, we played back and forth, lightly but firmly tossing our beliefs to and fro. I kept my calm. I respected his knowledge and status as the doctor and he in turn respected my knowledge and status as the mother. Finally, he relented.

"Okay", he said. "We will try weaning her. BUT, any evidence from the nurses that she is having a seizure, and she goes back on it."

"Thank you," I said calmly. Inwardly, I was elated. I immediately went over to tell Carla the good news. "Carla, here's the deal, honey. I am trying to get you off a very strong drug that is making you very sluggish. It is a drug I know you do not need anymore. Now you know the doctor thinks you should be on this drug so the nurses will be watching you carefully for any signs of twitching. That means you are having a seizure. You will also be having a test of your brain where they will put electrodes on your scalp. It will not hurt and the evidence from this test will also help determine if you need to be on this drug."

This was one of many conversations I would have with Carla. I would speak to her as the fully aware little being I knew she was. Whenever I spoke to Carla this way I could feel the thoughts of the medical staff around me. Why is she bothering to talk to her like that? I knew they thought our talks were silly and useless. But it really didn't matter to me what they thought. What mattered was that Carla was aware, and that everyone who interacted with her should communicate *somehow* what they were doing to her body and why.

I saw with gratitude how all the seminars and rebirthings I had been doing with Barbara and Glenn, my spiritual mentors, had prepared me to understand the spiritual and emotional nature of babies and how strongly they are influenced by everything and everyone around them. All I had learned would now be fully used.

Why do we think that just because babies can't communicate to us in words that they are ignorant of what is happening around them? It is appalling to speak negatively in the presence of babies as if they cannot understand. They may not understand the words, but they certainly do understand the *intent* and the *feeling* behind the words. This I believe to be true in my heart. So it was with a different awareness that I entered the medical world into which Carla was thrust. It was my job as Carla's mother to take as much care of her emotional being as they were taking care of her physical being.

Somehow we think because babies' bodies are physically immature, their spirits and emotions are incapable of awareness. When I spoke to Carla, I spoke with a mother's love to the full intelligence and full understanding that resided in her body. She needed to know that I was present. She needed to hear my reassuring voice. She needed to hear words of caring and support. That means so much to any baby's spiritual self. Babies must be spoken to with respect—the same respect you would give to an older child.

That weekend a different neonatologist was on duty. As soon as I saw him walk over to me I could feel his negativity. "You know, Mrs. Snyder, I think you need to realize some facts about Carla for now and for the future. You do know that your baby is going to be severely retarded and incapable of doing the simplest things?"

"Excuse me," I interjected, "If you are going to speak this way about my child we will have to move away from her bedside because I don't wish for her to hear what you are saying." I then physically removed myself from the bedside into a corner of the room. He followed and continued his message of how useless her life was going to be.

I had to stop him. I really didn't want to hear anymore. "Yes, I understand your point of view, but my husband and I think it is too early to say what will be."

It was so strange the way he was telling me all this. I felt that he was trying hard to bring me down to his level of hopelessness and some sort of strange, despairing acceptance. Of course, my refusal to hear the whole story of how awful Carla's life was going to be just got me labeled as the parent who was in denial. That is what the social worker would write down in the doctor's notes: "Mom in denial."

To me, all it meant was that there was disagreement between us. They solidly believed in the limitations and permanence of the damaged physical body. I just as strongly believed in the possibility of healing and limitless potential of the human body. And beyond that, I knew they were not the ones in ultimate control of this situation. God was.

Chapter 5

Carla's Victories

The ICU was not a fun place to spend my hours. Every morning I entered it split by dread and hope. I dreaded that there would be something else to worry about, yet I hoped that today there would be a change for the better. As Carla came off the phenobarbitol, she was more awake and made slight movements. However, there was still the big letdown—her suck and gag reflexes were missing. That meant she had no swallowing ability.

All day long, I would watch the nurses suction her mouth and nose with small plastic tubes. Because of her inability to swallow she was always at risk of secretions going into her lungs and of developing aspiration pneumonia or choking. I longed so much to put her to my breast and nurse her. I had to settle for having milk sucked out of my breasts several times a day by a breast pump. I had enough milk for the whole ward. Small amounts would be given to Carla by means of a tube down her nose into her belly. The amount had to be carefully monitored.

It was becoming apparent that she had a condition called reflux, where the food ingested comes back up. For Carla, who still could not swallow, that was always a danger. One night she started to turn dusky after a feed. She was taken off food and fed intravenously. Everything was up and down with her feedings, but at least she was gaining weight, and that was a good sign. Her biggest step forward came the day she could breathe without any oxygen assistance. The big ugly tube had come out of her throat at the end of the first week. Then the c-pap was removed. The c-pap was a plastic cannula that was taped over her nose; it had made her look like an anteater. Finally, she was weaned to room air.

By now we knew that the machine we really had to watch in Carla's case was the machine that monitored her oxygen levels. A little electrode wrapped around her toe or finger constantly displayed her oxygen level on a monitor. When she was in the nineties we knew she was doing well.

Now that several weeks had gone by, the things that Carla could *not* do really didn't matter anymore. She could not respond to light or noise; she had no grasp or body movements other than arching her body to the side; she made no noises whatsoever…Carla's brain had been so badly damaged at birth that all her basic body functions had been severely affected. They told us that she would be in a vegetative state of very limited movement. She would be unable to speak, cry, or smile.

We looked to every little thing she *could* do. She could pick up her head when on her stomach. She could breathe on her own. She could digest food. We chose to see each of these things as victories.

What they told us really didn't matter anymore because day after day we were falling more and more in love with Carla. She was my baby. She was beautiful. And that was all that mattered. All I wanted to do was get her through this hospital experience and home with the rest of us where she belonged. It was so hard to go home without her each night. It felt so terribly wrong.

Each night I would go out in the bitter cold to the parking lot and drive myself home. One of these nights the relentless pressure of events just welled up uncontrollably inside me. I sat in the car sobbing and cried out to God, "Why me God? What did I ever do to deserve this? Why do you hate me so?" Every sin of my past came whirling through my mind. But had I really done anything so horrendous that I deserved a child so ill, and a situation so complicated and stressful?

It would be a very long time before I would come to see all this not as punishment from God but as an opportunity and blessing. Only later would I be grateful for the lessons I would learn from my seriously disabled child.

Chapter 6

Every Day Blessings

"Would you like to give your baby a bath today?" Sue asked.

Would I ever! The idea thrilled me, but how could that be accomplished with all the gadgets and the intravenous line she was hooked up to? If Sue said it could it be done, however, I knew it was possible. From the beginning, when she encouraged us to believe Carla could survive pneumonia, I had complete faith in her. Now as time went on and we shared many hours together, I had the utmost faith in her. Sue was my dream of what a nurse should be. She was attentive, caring, and skillful. She performed all the meaningful gestures that made Carla much more comfortable. Sue remembered that her patients were not just names on a medical chart and that parents needed more than just diagnoses. Whenever she had Carla on the weekends, Bob and I would totally relax because we knew that for twelve hours on those two days, Carla was in the best of hands.

We had such camaraderie with her. Since we were there all day on the weekends we had plenty of time to talk with her about matters unrelated to Carla's condition. One day she and I got on the topic of how some husbands never seem to notice hairstyle changes on their wives. They might notice other women, especially attractive ones, but not always their wives. I told her laughingly of one time I not only had my hair color changed but cut much shorter than usual. When I walked in the house Bob looked right at me and started talking as if nothing was different. Or maybe it just looked so bad he didn't have the heart to say anything. Hair was definitely a topic of discussion with Sue. She liked change. Almost every weekend we saw something different—the color, the cut, a perm—something.

"Well," Sue said. "Do you want to make bets on Bob noticing my hair today? After all, it's curly from the permanent I just had."

I laughed, "Oh, on you he will definitely notice."

Bob walked over to us and took one look at Sue. "I see you changed your hair again," were his first remarks of the day. Sue and I both cracked up. It was no use trying to explain why to Bob. It was definitely a women's joke. It was just nice to have a few moments of lightness amidst everything else. Sue brought us that, and it was such a gift.

Until now, my greatest thrill had been to finally hold Carla, intravenous lines and all. But now the idea of giving her a bath—wow! At this point she had only one intravenous line in her neck, and her heart and breathing had stabilized, so it would be possible to bathe her. Sue brought a little pink plastic tub and in went Carla, water, and soap. She held her carefully as I washed her for the first time. "Carla, isn't this exciting? Your very first bath!" I gushed excitedly. And how long has it been, three weeks? In my heart, I thanked this nurse for helping me to have a normal experience with Carla, amidst everything else that was so painfully unnatural.

Others looked at us with some surprise. It wasn't every baby that got to have a bath in the ICU. But by this time, everyone knew Carla was an exceptional baby to her family and they were accustomed to seeing all of us at her bedside talking to her, holding her, and singing to her. As glad as I was to be with Carla, I felt bad for so many of the babies whose parents came to visit only briefly. One day a mom rushed in to see her little girl, stayed at her bedside a few minutes and prepared to leave.

"It's just too hard for me to see her like this. That's why I don't stay," she remarked to me as she was leaving.

"That's too bad," I thought in my head, "It's really hard for your baby to be here all day long all by herself."

Next to Carla was a sweet little girl, five months old, who had been born with her intestines inside out. Her parents never came. They did send clothes though. All of the nurses made an effort to speak to the baby. They felt bad for her, I'm sure. One day, one of the nurses confided that it was a good thing for Carla that we were here interacting with her. She said that babies that spent many months all by themselves very often had problems interacting properly in the future. Later I thought, "Why isn't this information provided to the parents?" As sick as some of these babies were, they needed to be spoken to, touched, and loved. All of these babies would use these experiences to build their future lives. How could any parent deny them?

There was one visitor all the babies had every day. It was the hospital's Catholic priest. He would stop briefly by each baby and say a prayer. Then just as quickly, he was gone. I would often add my own prayers and send them towards the babies. Religious people and rabbis were always allowed in the ICU. This was a city hospital, and by the end of two months I figured every denomination and then some had been represented.

If someone looked like he or she might be a religious person, my Aunt Edna was sure to use her gentle, convincing way to lure them over to Carla's bed for a prayer. And every one of them was kind enough to oblige her even when she mistakenly took a Hasidic Jew in his orthodox dress to be a rabbi and asked him for a blessing. I was so grateful to this man who kindly informed her that he was not a rabbi, but he would certainly come over and say a blessing. And a beautiful blessing he did bestow: that Carla would be loved and cherished by her family, and that she would be seen as a blessing to all. Little did he know how enduring his blessing would be...

Determining just what religion we were may have been a point of confusion for the staff. In Carla's crib were pictures of Jesus and of a holy man in India, Sai Baba, that a friend had given. I figured the more holy people with her, the better. I'm sure some questions were raised in some minds, but everyone was too polite to ask. Actually, one of the nurses told me that someone had asked if the picture of the Indian man was a picture of the baby's father. I thought that was a riot because Carla was as white as could be—with blue eyes and blond hair. Sai Baba is a very dark skinned man with a big bushy Afro.

The other point of confusion for the staff was just who Edna was—Bob's parent or my own? "Now we can't quite figure out who exactly is who's mother," one of the nurses asked one day in all seriousness.

"Oh no." I thought. "I have to wrangle my way out of this one." This is what happens when you lie; people keep asking questions and the hole that you dug gets deeper. Now these nurses were not stupid, of course. I had lied by giving my mother the dubious distinction of being my mother some days, and Bob's mother other days. After several weeks, most of them had seen me, Bob, my mother, and Edna enough to figure out which was my mother; we look very much alike. But they could not figure out how Edna could be Bob's mother because these two had no common characteristics at all. Zero. After the hell I had gone through regarding family members in the ICU, I was not about to add that Edna was my aunt and no one's mother. Soon, no more questions were asked. Maybe they just accepted the fact that another peculiarity of this family was that no one wanted to confess to being Bob's mother. And soon everyone came to love and adore Edna so much they couldn't care less who she was. They saw the devotion and love and all the late night hours she spent in the hospital with Carla.

Most people who spend any amount of time with my aunt, Edna, usually end up adoring and loving her. She is just the kind of person everyone likes. They enjoy listening to her stories and chatting with her. She takes the time and interest to talk to everyone—from the doctors to the janitors. The nurses even threw her a surprise birthday party, which surprised her so much, she cried. She is definitely the most likeable person in our family. And with good reason. There has been a special connection between Carla and Edna right from the beginning.

Chapter 7

Necessary Adjustments

"Mrs. Snyder, we need to talk," said the new doctor bluntly. Whenever someone said we needed to talk, my heart would pound, "What's wrong now?" I knew I could no longer put off this conversation. It had been six weeks, and Carla obviously was not going to be able to swallow or suck. This meant it was time to discuss surgery to insert a feeding tube directly into her stomach to provide nourishment. The doctor knew how strongly I opposed Carla having surgery, and I knew she had given her every chance to avoid it. I also knew how much Carla hated having a tube down her nose to feed her.

"You know," she said, "the sooner she has this done, the sooner she will be able to go home." Home—yes, home. It was the first time the possibility of going home had even been mentioned. The excitement of the thought immediately balanced out my dislike of Carla undergoing surgery.

"Okay," I said. "Then it will be done."

* * *

The next day, Bob and I had a meeting with the pediatric surgeon who would perform this surgery. We found our way over to the university hospital, parked, and walked up to her office. The doctor who would perform surgery on our baby was a very beautiful woman, elegantly dressed. She looked as if she had just stepped off the cover of Vogue. She was tall, slender, with dark hair pulled back, and not a strand out of place.

She explained that an opening would be made in Carla's stomach. A small plastic insert with a clamp would be permanently implanted. Through this tube we would feed her. It was called a gastrostomy tube, or G-tube. We, as parents, would learn how to change and take care of it.

Carla would also have another procedure done to help stop the reflux. Tucks would be made around the opening in the stomach so food would stay down. It all sounded horrible to us, like she wasn't really talking about the body of our daughter. To the doctor, it was obviously a routine procedure. I noticed that the whole time she spoke, she never made eye contact with us, or really looked at us at all. She spoke—as if to the walls. Maybe that was what surgeons did. Maybe it was a protective mechanism. If I had the responsibility of cutting into the body of a loved child, I might not want to look into her parents' eyes either. I might not want to see all that fear, all the love, all the hope.

I had heard from another mother in the ICU that this doctor did good work, that she was very result-oriented. That was enough to give us a measure of peace and confidence in this doctor who took our child's life into her hands.

The day of the surgery was hell. We set off with Carla for the OR, which was located in the basement of the hospital. All I could think of was that the morgue, too, was in the basement. My husband tightened his grasp of my hand. He knew how hard this was for me. We continued in silence and walked through the doors.

After we signed a few papers, a nurse came in to say a few words and off Carla went. I felt the anguish of her being taken away again. I tried not to think about her body being cut open, tried to push away the thought, "What if she doesn't make it through this?"

It was a long four hours. We sat in the coffee shop across from each other, poking at our food. What do parents say to each other when their child is having surgery? There just wasn't much need for words. We could only wonder at how this all happened to our child. It was difficult to erase the mental image of the doctor cutting into our daughter, of tubes being inserted, Carla unconscious through it all. I had no idea how it was going. Was everything routine? Was anything new being discovered? We had to put our trust in the doctor, and in God and his angels to watch over Carla and bring her through this.

Finally, it was over. We were told that everything had gone smoothly, and Carla was back up in the ICU bed. We could see her.

It was a shock to look at her body. Long, ugly stitches were drawn vertically across her stomach. Her skin was discolored. I was unnerved when I went over to touch her and let her know I was there. The moment I did so, I knew intuitively that something was wrong. She didn't seem quite right to me. Luckily, the nurse who was attending her didn't think so either and took her blood pressure.

"Her blood pressure is very high," the nurse said. "I will notify the doctor. This means she is in pain and will need more pain medication to relax her body." For once I wanted drugs in her body as quickly as possible. I could only imagine how painful it must have felt. Carla didn't cry, so the nurse had used the blood pressure to know if she was in pain. Despite all the procedures done on her, Carla never once cried or whimpered in the ICU. It would be many months before she would be able to make any verbal acknowledgments of pain.

The next day she was ready to be fed with her new tube. I watched in amazement as the milk flowed easily down the tube into her belly. There would be no more tubes down her nose; no more intravenous feeding. This was easy by comparison. I very quickly got over my aversion to the tube in her belly. Although it was hard to see a plastic tube sticking out of her healthy pink flesh, the tube belonged there and it served an important purpose. It was part of her for now. Everything would be easier, and the tube did not have to stay in forever. Most importantly, we would soon be taking her home.

Chapter 8

Coming Home

"Okay. Today you're going to learn how to suction Carla," said the nurse. "The tube is used to suction both the nose and the mouth."

I knew it was something I had to learn. I had seen it done hundreds of times. Yet something within me hesitated to actually try it. Because Carla could not swallow, she had to be suctioned several times an hour, sometimes more, sometimes less. There were times when I wondered where all the secretions could possibly come from—she had so much mucus. Doing the mouth was not so bad. But to go down her nose—my heart started beating faster in fear of hurting her.

"You have to angle it slightly once you hit the back of the nose, and then go down to where the red mark appears on the tubing," the nurse showed me. I inserted the tubing, got to the back of her nose, felt the hardness, and couldn't get beyond a feeling of violating Carla's body. I tried the other nostril. I couldn't do that one either. I could feel myself start to sweat. I had to learn how to do this. A few more attempts with the nurse coaxing me, and down it went. I suctioned quickly and withdrew the tubing.

What a strange feeling. There was no choice in the matter. It had to be done. Once I got over the fear, it felt good to be able to take an active part in Carla's care. It made me feel better…a more significant part of her life.

In no time Bob and I were pros. "Good job," the nurse said, marking it down in her book. Everything they taught us had to be documented.

Finally the big day arrived. We were actually going to take Carla home. I was so elated and excited! Carla had recovered beautifully from her surgery. She had gained weight and maintained her ability to breathe independently. Everything was a go! She was coming home with two pieces of machinery: a heart monitor and an oxygen level monitor called a pulsoximeter.

Many of the nurses came over to wish us a warm good-bye. The first neonatologist we had met, Dr. Rack, came over and said his farewell. I thought that was a special touch. Later, my mother would tell of a conversation she had with him the last day. He told her how impressed he was by the way we all pitched in to take care of Carla. I didn't make much of that statement until I sadly realized that what we had done was a rarity. No other family had taken that much time to be with their baby. The hospital staff must have perceived us as an exception, not the norm.

I bundled Carla into her new pink snowsuit. For a few minutes I was just another parent taking her baby home from the hospital for the first time. The first important person for Carla to meet waited outside the ICU. Anora, her big sister of four, had not seen Carla for all these eight weeks. I brought Carla right over to where Bob was waiting with her. "Look, Anora. It's your very own baby sister."

Anora was a little bewildered at the commotion of nurses and people, but she managed to give Carla a big smile. At four, she had the face of a cherub, all sweetness. When she smiled, her eyes seemed to disappear into those squeezeable cherub cheeks, and her short, light brown hair, framed her face. She sat with Carla that day filled with the shyness and curiosity of any four-year-old. Anora would prove to be the best of all big sisters, for sure. It was at this moment that Carla became a real part of Anora's world, and Anora welcomed her.

"It's a whole new beginning for you, sweetheart. You are going to your very own home where we can be with you all the time," I whispered to Carla on the way home. "Everything is going to be better now."

I planned a big welcome home party for Carla's second night with us. I wanted to make a special occasion of her homecoming. My husband made up a huge WELCOME HOME CARLA sign. We had balloons, friends, family, and food. I was ecstatic. Finally I had Carla away from the negativity and routine of the ICU and into her warm loving home. I was almost giddy with happiness and relief from being out of the hospital environment. It had taken so much out of me to have to be there every day. Now, within the walls of our home with our two daughters, all was as it should be.

Carla slept through her whole party. My mother sat in a chair holding her granddaughter proudly almost the whole time. Carla wore a pretty pink dress, looking like any other newborn in a grandma's arms. The rest of us had a good time, speaking optimistically of what lay ahead. Everyone said she looked beautiful. I was exuberant for her future now that she was safely at home. We shared many stories of how babies like Carla had survived the odds to become healthy children. One friend shared a story about a woman who was told her son was severely retarded and that he would never amount to anything. Instead of giving up, she devised her own way of teaching him and he succeeded through her devotion. That story stuck in my mind.

My high-pitched exuberance was soon replaced with the realities of the day-to-day care of a baby with special needs. We needed to find a nighttime nurse—and quick. Because Carla could never be alone, we had to take turns staying up with her throughout the night. Even at night she had to be suctioned, and every four hours she had to be tube-fed, which involved more than the usual preparation. She also had to be thumped on her back and sides every few hours to loosen any secretions. It was more than we could handle on our own, so we quickly got out the lists of nursing agencies and made calls. Luckily, our insurance company was allowing us eight hours a night of nursing care. Amen.

In a few more nights we welcomed our first night nurses. One attended Carla for the duration of the week and one stayed over the weekend. It was the beginning of a long string of nurses. Some would be a blessing, some would be a challenge, and some would be a nightmare.

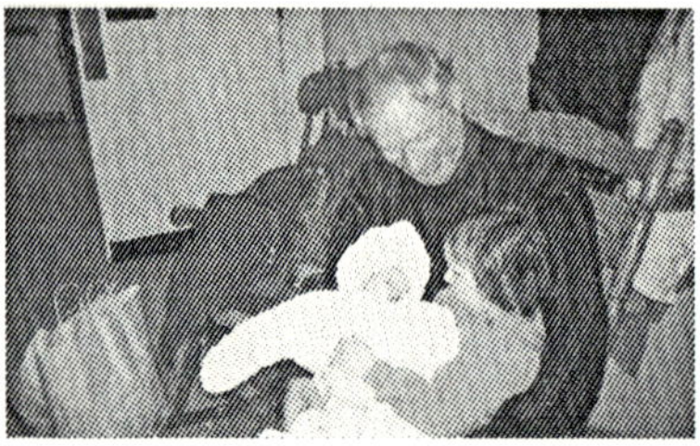

Anora, the big sister, seeing Carla for the first time after 2 months, with Dad

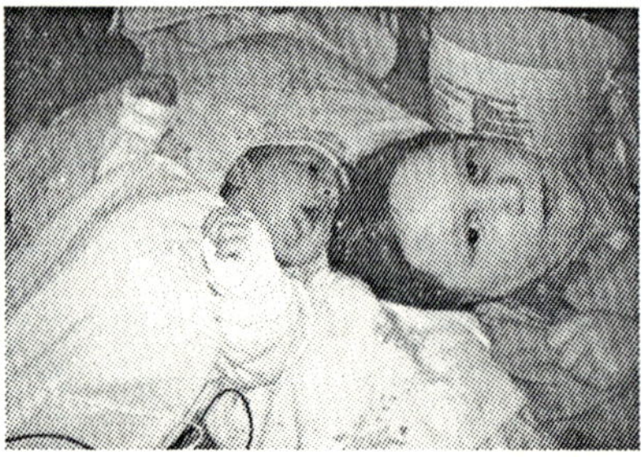

The first day at home together for Carla and Anora. Anora, not so sure yet about this new little person

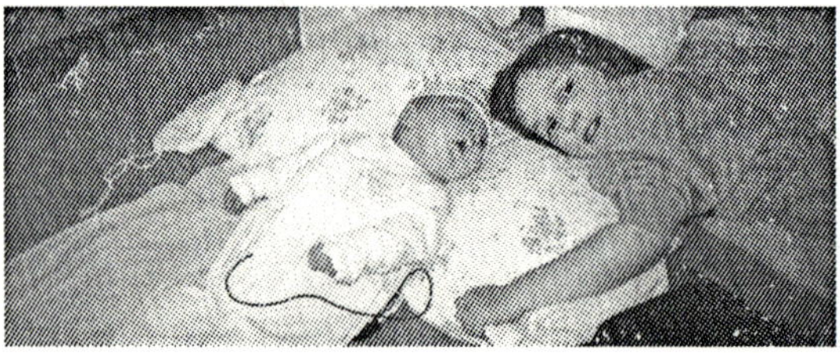

Anora deciding yes! she does like her little sister

Ashley, my stepdaughter's child, and future helper with Carla's special program

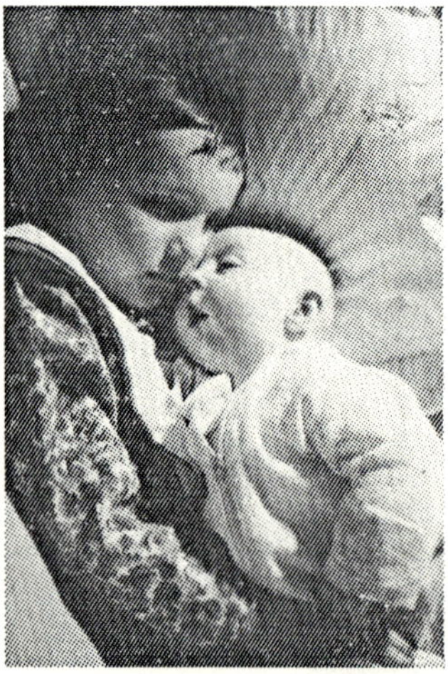

Anora in one of her frequent snuggles with Carla

The nurses in the Intensive Care Unit surprised us by helping Carla create endearing Valentines

Chapter 9

Emergency

In my early dealings with hired nurses, I naively assumed that the agencies would only send competent nurses who were qualified to assist us in the special care of Carla, and who would be more knowledgeable than we were about her medical conditions. Soon enough we would learn that this was a business, and the business was to fill the slots up with whoever was available.

But these first two nurses seemed caring and competent and we were grateful to be able to sleep at night again. Carla was soon taken off the cardiac monitor and was only hooked up at night to the pulsoximeter, her oxygen measuring device. A tiny little electrode was wrapped around her big toe. If the level of her oxygen went below a certain number it would beep loudly. Then she would either have to be suctioned, or repositioned, or just looked at to determine whether or not she was just in a deep sleep. I would hear the beep go off several times a night and lie there waiting for the nurse to take care of Carla. As soon as the beep had stopped I would relax and go back to sleep.

Carla's room was our living room. Luckily, it was big enough to hold her and all her apparatus and still have room for us to move. Next to her bassinet that any baby would sleep in was a cart that held all her medical supplies. To the right of her was a little table with her pulsox machine, and on the floor was the suction machine. Off in the corner were two oxygen tanks in case of emergency. We put a children's wardrobe nearby with her clothing, and that is where she lived. Our bedroom was right off the living room, so I could hear all that was going on at night and know if everything was alright.

At first I had a fantasy of having Carla sleep in bed with me so I could snuggle her. I felt she had been so deprived of that in the hospital. Halfway through the first night it was obvious this was not going to work. She had to be repositioned constantly for optimum breathing and suctioned every hour, her machines would go off…there wasn't any way I was going to get any sleep. The nurse was nice to try, kind enough not to say right off, "This isn't going to work!" But it had been worth the effort, if only to know that it wasn't possible. There would be enough nights in the future when a nurse wouldn't show up that I would be able to sleep right next to Carla on the living room floor.

Four weeks had gone by and we were getting the routine down. Carla seemed to be stable. Then she had a stretch of a few days where she started sleeping more, she was quieter, her mucus started getting thicker. I didn't think too much of it and the nurses who took her vital signs and listened to her lungs didn't say anything was wrong. We hoped it was just a cold her body would work through. This would be our first lesson that what other babies routinely survived on their own, Carla could not.

By now I was trusting her night nurses and their medical knowledge. But the next morning when I woke up and went to say good morning to Carla, I knew something was wrong. I noticed her color wasn't good and she was breathing much faster than normal. "Tiksha," I asked her nurse, "Isn't Carla's breathing awful fast?"

"Oh no," she answered, unconcerned. "Babies sometimes breathe fast." Tiksha was getting ready to leave. Her eleven to seven shift was over.

As soon as she left, I bundled Carla up and told my husband, "I'm taking Carla over to that walk-in doctor's office. I don't like the way Carla is breathing, and she is too pale."

In the office, I told the receptionist that my baby was not breathing right and asked if we could be seen soon. The next thing I knew a nurse came our way, took one look at Carla and we were whisked into an examination room. The doctor arrived, listened to Carla's lungs, saw her rapid breathing. One look at his face and I knew Carla was in trouble. All the rest happened in a fast, frightening blur of activity.

This was obviously a young, fairly new doctor with a real emergency on his hands, and he handled it well. Without panicking, he told me Carla was in acute respiratory distress with pneumonia. The EMT team was on its way over to put the tube down into her lungs again and she would be flown via helicopter to a hospital with a pediatric intensive care unit.

Back to an intensive care unit, back onto a ventilator, a case of pneumonia again—I could barely take it all in. How could all this be happening again so soon? I was terrified of the prospect of Carla having to fly all alone. I asked if I could go with her in the helicopter. No, I was not allowed. I could meet her at the hospital, which fortunately was only half an hour away.

"Carla, you are going to have your first flight. I can't go with you, but I will be in the car and be at your side as soon as I can," I consoled Carla as they were preparing her for departure. I called my husband, told him to call Edna, and off I flew down the highway praying all the while with my heart pounding.

In the emergency room, a young resident came over to take all the details of Carla's history. She was so agonizingly slow. All I wanted to do was see Carla. These questions, although I knew they were vital for the doctor's knowledge of her case, were the last thing I wanted to deal with. When could I see Carla? She explained patiently that a series of tests were being done right now. I hated being in yet another hospital. What would I encounter in this one?

Edna arrived. We hugged and waited outside the door of the ICU together. Every moment was like an eternity of not knowing what was being done to my daughter and wondering how she was doing.

Finally, they came for me. Carla had a room all her own. There she was with the all-too-familiar tubing down her mouth and into her chest to breathe for her. There she was with IV's again. The nurse explained a few things to me and said the doctor would be in shortly. It was not a long wait until the doctor came in. She was a small Indian woman and she had a no-nonsense air about her. She also had a weary look—as if she had seen too much.

She told me Carla had pneumonia—that her situation was serious. She was not optimistic about her recovery given the results of her blood tests. She wanted to do a spinal tap. I was about to go into my objections when I stopped. Something told me, "Don't say no, don't give this woman objections. This is a totally different situation." It was agonizing for me to think of Carla having to go through one more painful thing, but I signed the permission form.

The next morning we had a conference in the atrium, a huge room right outside the intensive care unit. Carla's "team" was all there: Edna, Bob, myself, and my friend, Barbara. The doctor spoke to us of Carla's condition and asked a lot of questions. She had a certain attitude about her, but I was oblivious to what was going on. Finally, she departed, leaving us all alone.

Barbara's eyes were of the clearest blue. With a penetrating gaze, she summoned my attention. "Did you notice, Cindy, how many questions she asked of you? I think she was trying to find out a lot about how you were taking care of Carla. I think she was trying to find out if Carla had been abused."

The word made me flinch. Abused? How could this doctor possibly think we had abused Carla? The thought never crossed my mind. Well, of course it hadn't. We all loved and cared for Carla. But Barbara had worked with abused children before, and was more aware of what had just transpired. She knew what the digging questions were for and recognized their progression in the search for that kind of information. She could probably read the doctor's suspicion of us.

"How could she possibly think that about us?" I asked.

"This doctor doesn't know you from Adam. Remember, Cindy, all she knows is a seriously sick baby comes to her. God only knows how many atrocities and neglect she has seen before in this city hospital," Barbara replied.

"What a horrible position for her to have to be in," I thought. It was a huge responsibility to figure out not only how to provide medical help to a child, but to have to figure out if a child had been abused. While I didn't like being put in a position of such suspicion, I understood the doctor's protocol. She was just doing her job.

Later that evening I looked around Carla's room wondering where I could sleep that night. I noticed a large chair in the corner. I asked the nurse, "Is that big chair where a parent could sleep?" There had been no overnight facilities to speak of in the other hospital, but this single room looked more promising.

"Oh no," she said in a shocked tone. "Parents aren't allowed to sleep in here." At the authoritative tone of her voice I could feel my blood pressure start to rise. I knew a confrontation was coming.

"Oh no?" I feigned surprise. "Well, I am most definitely staying here tonight. Sleeping in that chair in the corner I will not be in anyone's way." I was not going to be away from Carla this time. My decision was made.

"Well, you can't," she stated flatly.

"Well I am."

"Mrs. Snyder, if that is your attitude, then I will have to inform the head nurse that you are breaking the rules."

"You just go right ahead and tell her," I almost spit the words out I was so angry.

Sure enough, a few minutes later, a head nurse showed up and proceeded to tell me what the rules were.

I had my strength this time as I looked her straight in the face. I said, "I am not leaving no matter what you say or do. There is no logical reason why I cannot stay here with my daughter, who is seriously ill." She took a good look at me, saw she was not going to break or change me, and left. Later as I walked down the hall I noticed another parent, in another room, sleeping in the chair in the corner.

Two days later, Carla was already showing major signs of improvement, much to the doctor's surprise. But not to mine. All day long I would be at Carla's bedside talking to her, touching her, and telling her how strong she was. This would prove to be a recurring scenario: Carla would get very sick, scare all the doctors into thinking she was dying, and then do a big turnaround and get better. She probably just wanted to get the hell out of the hospital.

The next day she was taken off the ventilator. Now I knew we had turned the corner. Preparations were made for her to go upstairs to the regular pediatric ward since she no longer needed intensive care. That move turned out to be both a blessing and a curse. In the intensive care unit she had meticulous one-on-one attention. But up in the pediatric ward a few nurses tended too many children. I knew she would not be properly suctioned with nurses coming in and out only occasionally. I was glad I was there day and night with Carla, making sure she was properly cared for. At least here, beds were available for parents in the room. There was even a shower down the hall.

Carla got most of her nursing care from me. I joked at the end of the week to my husband that I was going to send the hospital a bill. I could see that they did not have the staff to provide as much time as I had spent with Carla. Or maybe once they figured out how competent I was at taking care of her, they slacked off.

I was the one who also caught an IV before it went bad and caused a problem. After the resident had tried unsuccessfully to get an IV in her arms, they finally put one in her thigh. Two days later I noticed her leg looked a little puffy. I called the nurse to take a look. He quickly did so and said it looked fine. A couple of hours later, I looked again, and this time it was even more swollen. This time I didn't bother with the nurse. I got the doctor. She looked at it and removed it immediately. I didn't want to consider what might have happened if I hadn't caught it. After several more days, Carla was pronounced well, and we went home.

Chapter 10

Defining Our Standard of Care

We were faced with another realization. If I was to go back to work, and Carla and Anora were to receive proper care, we would need more help at home. We were finding out the huge amount of work involved in raising a seriously brain-injured child.

I had gone back and forth on the issue of returning to my chiropractic practice. My colleague, Mariangela, and my right hand assistant, Sandy, were doing a miraculous job keeping the practice going, but my patients were wondering when I would return. Once we obtained an additional eight hours a day of nursing care for Carla there was no reason for me not to go back to my three-day workweek.

Our new nurse worked from 7 in the morning until 3 in the afternoon. I didn't know enough to interview her personally, so, I never asked her how she felt about brain-injured children or determined her attitude towards their care. Her feelings would be revealed soon enough.

Bob didn't like this new nurse from the start. She was overweight, and not especially energetic or cheerful. I dismissed his dislike as prejudice against overweight nurses. Bob felt that nurses should manage themselves well because they were educated to provide care. He felt that their self-care was a partial measure of how well they were capable of applying their training. I would soon learn not to dismiss Bob's intuitive feelings. He was right about the nurses every time. Soon, I could see that she was not able to get up and down from the floor easily with Carla to do some of the activities designed to stimulate her. More important than her physical limitations was the vague feeling I was starting to have of her just not being so great around Carla.

Besides this nurse, a local woman, Theresa, came in several times a week to help us with the household. Theresa was an efficient woman with dark hair and a husky, smoker's voice. She had been rather timid when she first came to work for us. But she knew our philosophy of thinking positively and doing the best for Carla, and she, too, was concerned for Carla's well being. She helped us out tremendously in keeping our household functioning.

"You know," she said in passing one day. "I was a little disturbed at the nurse the other day."

"Oh really?" I said calmly. "What did she do?"

"You know how you and Bob have stressed how important it is to be doing stimulating things for Carla with all those exercises? The other day when neither you or Bob were home I noticed Carla wide-awake and the nurse sitting there reading a book, ignoring Carla. So I asked her, 'Don't the Snyders want you to be doing things with Carla when she is awake?'

"Well she just gave me a look like I was stupid and said, 'Don't you know it isn't worth the time to do anything with Carla? She is too badly brain damaged for anything to help.'"

I thought I would explode when Theresa was finished. "Thanks Theresa," I managed to get out. "I am really glad you told me this." That was the final straw. That nurse would never step foot in my house again. I ran to the phone, got a hold of the supervisor at the agency and told her that nurse was not to show up in my house tomorrow or any other day—ever. My voice was shaking with anger as I explained to her we did not appreciate having someone with such a mentality in our house. There was no sympathy or attempt to understand on the other end of the phone. A replacement would be sent as soon as possible.

Respect for Carla was something I was absolutely committed to, and this nurse had grossly violated that respect. While she and all the doctors thought Carla was severely retarded, I never believed it for a moment. When I first saw "severely retarded" written in the doctor's notes, I wondered, "How could they make a diagnosis of retardation at six months?" As time went on I knew Carla was very aware of her environment and the people in it. She was a very alert little being who just could not express herself as other babies could or move her body the way other babies could. There was no doubt that she knew me and others in the family. I had no way to prove it. I just knew it. I viewed intelligence as potential, and I wondered at the professionals who made assumptions about my child when they spent so little time actually being with her. At first it irked me; gradually I would let it go. Many people could not relate to a child who did not fit the image of an average child, or communicate in the average way. It was a prejudice that I, too, experienced before Carla came into my life.

Our experience with a bad nurse was soon to change with a wonderful new daytime nurse, Joanne. She would stay with us for almost a year. Joanne had a certain exuberance about her. She was short. Her brown hair was lovely, long and curly. And she had expressive warm brown eyes. She was young, intelligent, capable, and best of all, she adored Carla. She had recently married and already looked forward to the joy of having her own baby. We soon came to relax and trust Carla alone in her presence.

Joanne had a sense of humor too. If she walked by a mirror holding Carla, she would stop and say, "Don't I look good with a baby in my arms?" Whenever we had to go to the pediatrician's office she would scrutinize everything the nurse was doing. Everything had to be done just right. Joanne was looking out for Carla too.

Whenever Carla was sick, Joanne would truly be upset. I guess that broke a rule of nursing, but Joanne couldn't help but break it—she cared. Going to the pediatrician's office so frequently was a new experience for me. With my other daughter, Anora, I had rarely gone to the medical doctor because she was never sick. But Carla's health was so precarious that after the first frightening experience, I took her immediately at the sign of any abnormality. In the beginning months I also thought the medical doctors would have other answers for me regarding what we could do to help Carla get better. Even with my strong belief and experience in alternative medicine, I thought this unusual situation would prompt some creative answers from the medical community. Bit by bit I discovered not only that they had no answers, but that medical doctors, in their ignorance, felt that if they did not have answers, no one else did either.

Our local hospital was the first place we went for an evaluation and treatment plan. Carla was noted to have a grasp reflex. Her excessive backward arching was now replaced with flaccid, floppy muscle tone. Her arms would occasionally jerk forward, and she could lift her head up for a few seconds while on her belly. Occasionally she would roll over. The result of this evaluation was to have Carla graded at the level of a newborn without the ability to cry, suck or swallow. Carla was now six months old.

Two therapists made home visits. The first showed us how to prop her up and taught us additional exercises intended to expose Carla to various textures and noises. She brought along a catalog of equipment for cerebral palsied children. The other therapist talked about Carla's vision. It was assumed Carla was blind. So she brought pamphlets about blind children. I felt this was something to deal with in the future. Right now what was important was to get her to learn how to swallow and to strengthen the occasional weak suck she had. They showed me how to stimulate the inside of her mouth and press against her hard palate. Sometimes I would be encouraged when I could feel a slight suck sensation.

The next week they called me up excitedly to recommend that I bring Carla over. A specialist in the sucking reflex was visiting and she would see Carla. "Oh, maybe this person will have an answer, a clue that has been overlooked by others," I thought. With anticipation, I brought Carla to her for an exam. Five minutes into it, I knew it was a waste of time. This specialist told me nothing new and recommended nothing different.

I was starting to feel frustrated. Surely someone somewhere knew how to help Carla. As nice as all the therapists and pediatricians were, we were making no headway.

I had not run out of hope in medicine—not yet. At our next pediatric visit I asked the doctor about going to some sort of specialized hospital for Carla.

"Yes I can recommend a doctor—a well known neurologist at a specialized hospital in Philadelphia," he said. "It will be a good idea for you to go."

"Good," I said gladly. "Give me a name and I will give a call." Little did I know what a traumatic event this would turn out to be.

Chapter 11

The Right Intention

"Barbara, we are going to a special hospital for kids to have a neurologist examine Carla. Would you like to come?"

"Let me come with you," she replied unhesitatingly.

Through all these months I had been on the phone many a time with Barbara for comfort and advice. Barbara was a role model for me as a woman. She was strong, yet entirely feminine. She won her way with reason and gentle persuasion. Her inner and outer beauty were an equal match.

Years ago, I participated in a special weekend organized by Barbara and her husband. It was a cathartic weekend—the beginning of my spiritual journey back to God, and it led to a completely different way of looking at my life. I didn't realize at the time that it also prepared me to become a stronger person; someone willing and able to take on a task such as becoming the mother of a profoundly brain-injured child. All the seeds had been sown to prepare me as I continued doing spiritual and self-improvement work with the *Alivening Project.* I had been learning about commitment, responsibility, trust, and about being in partnership with your spouse and with God.

Off to Philadelphia we went—Bob, Barbara, Anora, and myself. We had a map with us, but somehow we found ourselves on the wrong side of the city. Finally, we found the place—a small relief for us all.

By now I was accustomed to visiting different hospitals. They were each starting to look the same. We found our way upstairs and sat in the small overcrowded waiting room. It was one of the sections that had not yet been renovated and it was old and shabby looking, not what I expected of such a prestigious hospital.

Finally, it was our turn. Bob and I walked in. I was full of expectation, certain that we were finally going to receive some helpful information. The doctor scooped up Carla, placed her on the exam table and in a matter of minutes had finished his exam and put her back in my arms. "Wait a minute," my mind said, "Isn't there more to the exam than this?"

"Tell me, what kind of educational background do you and your husband have?" were his first words to us. His question jolted me. What did our education have to do with this? We both spoke of our advanced degrees. As if not hearing our replies he asked, "Do you have her CT scans?"

"Yes right here. Here they are."

"Let's go and look at them."

I followed him to another room with X-ray viewboxes. Bob went to be with Anora, who was getting restless. The doctor put Carla's films up, looked at them and turned to me. "Her brain is all full—of edema. There is fluid here, where the brain cells should be." The impact of what he was saying robbed me of my next breath.

"What the hell are you saying," my mind screamed, "... my daughter has no brain?"

He led me back to the exam room. Barbara got up to come with me. He wanted to know who she was. Then he launched into his verdict. "The most your daughter will ever be able to do is roll from side to side. None of her present capabilities will ever improve. She will have serious respiratory problems. This is considering the fact of course, that she will probably not live past the age of seven."

His words stung. They were so stark, so cold. There was no feeling behind the dismal picture he was painting. The possibility she might not even live past seven kept echoing in my brain. I had never thought Carla would be given a death sentence. No one had been that explicit before.

The next thing I knew I was on my feet leaving that room as quickly as I could. I was at the receptionist's desk paying a huge fee—I wondered, "For what?" For the quickest exam ever? for the most impersonal treatment ever? for the worst prognosis ever? The enormity of what he had said hung on me for several hours. My body literally felt crushed. Bit by bit, I began to shake it off.

"Remember, it is just one person's opinion," Barbara said.

"I know, but I really thought this doctor of such renown was going to be the one to give me hope. He gave me just the opposite." On our way home, the further we traveled from the hospital the lighter we became about the whole scene, juxtaposing it with our hopes for Carla.

Fortunately, that evening, a mutual healer friend of Barbara's and mine was in town, and we were headed there. It was the complete opposite of the environment we had left behind. This healer worked on another realm—a spiritual realm. And were we ever ready for that after our day! We walked tiredly into the office where Laura was seeing patients that night. "How was your day?" Laura asked.

We told her every horrible thing that had happened. Soon, the heaviness of the morning was leaving our bodies. I felt normal again. Gratefully, I handed Carla to Laura. With loving concern, she began her work. Her straight blonde hair draped over Carla as she leaned over her closely. Laura was not of small stature, but she moved effortlessly around Carla, working with her energy fields in the Reiki tradition. She moved her hands around her body and touched her gently at several points. What a difference it made to be with someone who cared, who believed in the body, in the possibility of healing!

I did not fully understand what she was doing, I just knew it was being done with the right intention, and with love. I watched Laura doing her work and prayed this would help Carla. I wanted so desperately for someone to make all the difference for her.

Little did I realize that soon I, myself, would be called upon to do what I never believed I was capable of doing for Carla.

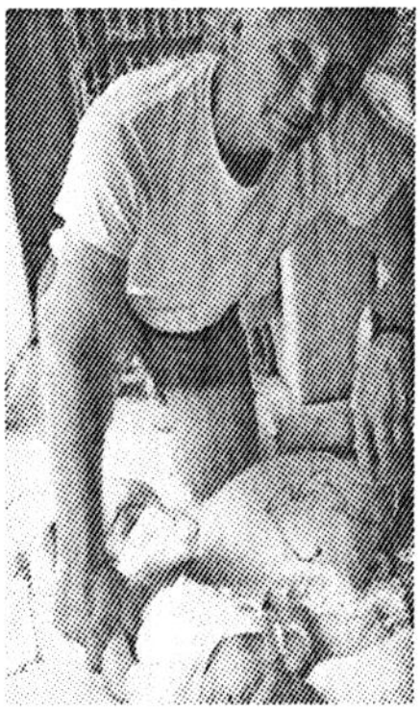

Dad—Bob, on diaper detail with Carla

Grandmother, Claire, in a quiet moment with Carla

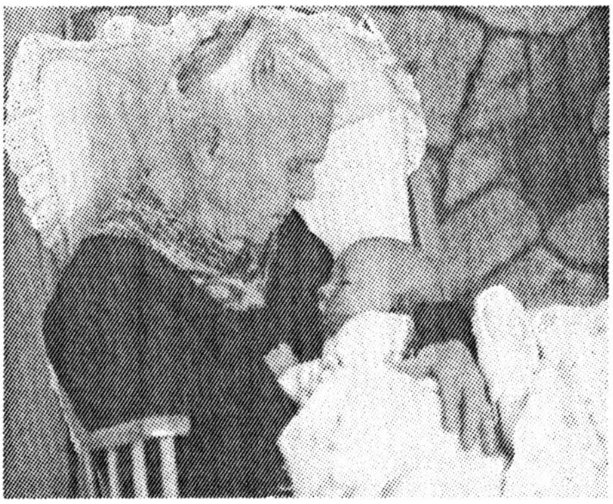

Edna, holding Carla gently and singing to her as she naps

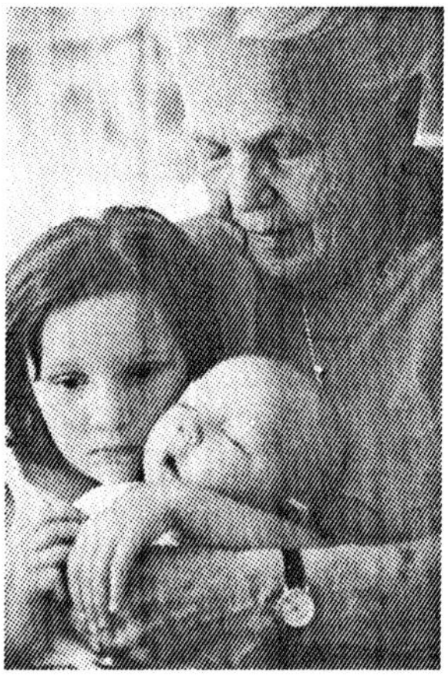

Anora, Carla, and Edna, all together at home

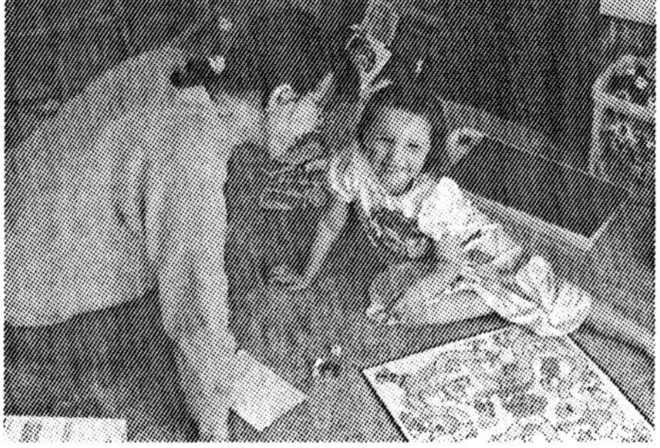

Mom—Cindy, and Anora, taking time out for a game together

Chapter 12

Nourishment: Growing into a New Feeding Tube

Bob, Anora, and my mom were headed off to our annual winter vacation in Florida. I was quite fine staying behind with Carla, especially after a disastrous phone call I had made to the social worker at the hospital. I had thought of calling the hospital to find out if there was a place I could leave Carla for a week so the rest of us could go away.

Innocently, I called the social worker at our hospital. She was the one who had that sort of information. I told her my thoughts of going away and asked whether she knew if any such facility existed.

"Why yes, Mrs. Snyder, there are places you could put Carla. And I'm sure she would be well taken care of." Then she lowered her voice an octave and proceeded in a placating tone, "You know, Mrs. Snyder, in situations like yours, it is not unusual for parents to permanently place their children in facilities. It is understood how difficult it is to have such a child."

I was floored. Wait a minute. All I asked for was a week, and she was suggesting a lifetime! "No," I replied tersely, "I would never consider such a situation for my child. We are very capable of taking care of her." When I hung up I was still reeling from the suggestion she had made.

To me, it was as if she had mentioned killing my child. Putting Carla away somewhere would be the same to me. It would be hell, and it was not an option.

That conversation did serve a useful purpose however. I became very clear I did not want to leave Carla in any home away from the home she knew. We decided that Edna would come and stay with me. I was sure we would have no problems. Carla had been stable again.

I was glad my family could go and do what we always did. Edna and my mother were both constant visitors at my house, helping us in every way they could with Carla. Edna would hold Carla for hours on end when she was sleeping. We had our routine down. As soon as Carla showed any signs of tiring, into Edna's arms she would go. Into the rocking chair. I would arrange the blankets around Carla, put a pillow behind Edna's arms, and put the stool next to the rocking chair. On the stool would go a cup of tea and any goodies I had. And there they would sit for two hours, sometimes even more. I don't know how Edna's bottom could survive sitting that long. But she would be busy talking to Carla, telling her about the wonders of nature or singing her German songs.

Sometimes I would peek at them. Carla would have such a wonderfully relaxed look on her face. I know these were moments of peace for her. Moments of peace in between the tube feedings, the suctioning of her mouth and nose, the pounding on the back, the frequent repositionings. I would only interrupt them if I thought Carla needed suctioning.

Once when Edna was holding her, I came over to see if Carla's feet were warm enough. They always seemed to be ice cold no matter how many socks I put on her. Finding them cold, I took one sock off at a time, and gently massaged her feet. At the same time Edna was holding and rubbing her hands. I looked up at her and said, "Well, isn't this a spoiled baby, having both ends massaged? Do you think she gets enough attention?" We both laughed. That's how it was when we took care of Carla. We wanted to spoil her and care for her in every way possible.

My husband had his own way of spoiling her too. Whenever he put her down for a nap he would keep rubbing her back until she was asleep. I hadn't realized how much she counted on that back rub until one day I put her down on her stomach for a nap and covered her as usual. She seemed very tired so I waited for her to fall asleep. Instead, her little head kept popping up as if she was trying to say something. Finally it dawned on me. "Oh—you want your back rub, don't you darling?" I laughed. I rubbed her back and she settled down.

It was a pleasure to take care of Carla. Sometimes it felt like a privilege. Every baby is so dependent on its mother. And Carla being a special baby, was even more dependent on me for so much. Because she was able to do less, I wanted to do more for her. One night I found out how much I was actually capable of being and doing for Carla. I discovered I could function in what I then perceived to be a crisis.

Carla's G-tube had been working fine. Since she never cried when she was hungry, we kept to a recommended every-four-hour, around-the-clock feeding. One night I had gone to bed, leaving Carla in the hands of our night nurse. Around three o'clock there was an insistent knock at my door. I knew something was wrong.

"Mrs. Snyder, Carla's G-tube has come out!"

"What do you mean her G-tube has come out? That is not supposed to happen!" I went out to the living room to see her G-tube totally deflated out of the opening into her belly. It was not a good sight to see. A G-tube is a long piece of brown tubing. Several inches of it stays inserted into the belly, and about eight inches lays outside the body. A little inflated balloon keeps it inside the stomach. The balloon had deflated, and the inside part had come out.

"Well you're a nurse. Why can't you put another one in?" I was thinking fast.

"Oh no, I am only a LPN. We are not allowed to put G-tubes back in. You have to be an RN to do that." I could see the fear on her perfectly made-up face.

Now I was starting to panic. I tried remembering what they had told us about the tube in the hospital. What I could remember them saying was that another had to be inserted soon or the opening would close up. The G-tube was her lifeline. It was how she got her nourishment. It had to be replaced right away. It struck me that they had not taught us how to insert G-tubes. How did that happen?

Edna appeared on the scene. "What's the problem?"

"The problem is her G-tube. It's come out, and another has to go back in." I tried not to sound as panic-stricken as I felt. I knew it was up to me. I was the one who had to do it. At that moment I knew I was the one who was going to come through for Carla. I started praying. "Please! Dear God, help me with this. I need your help to do this right." I found a package with a new tube, took it out, and remembered the first step was to lubricate the end with KY jelly. Meanwhile, I slipped on a pair of sterile gloves.

I felt like a surgeon. For me, inserting a tube into my daughter's belly was unfamiliar territory. I looked for the line that showed how far to insert it. The thought of sticking this tube into her belly made me weak.

"Carla, sweetie, I have to put a tube into your belly. I don't want to hurt you, honey, but it might feel a little strange going in." Carla just lay there quietly. I felt more nervous doing this procedure for the first time than I did when I first learned to suction the back of her nose. Into the belly it went. The nurse and Edna watched me wordlessly. Then I filled the five cc syringe with water to inflate the balloon which kept it inside. The last thing was to pull on it, making sure it was secure. I didn't relish doing that either. I did it. It was fine. I had done it. "Thank you God," I said over and over. "Thank you for your help."

Edna, turned to me with a soft, appreciative gaze. "You were really praying hard weren't you?" That was an understatement.

All these things that would soon become normal and routine were initially so traumatic for me. But seeing that I could do them gave me an enormous sense of accomplishment. I could do whatever was needed to keep Carla alive and well.

* * *

There was something important about G-tubes that we had not been told. No one told us that after so many months she would need a larger tube. Through all our visits to local pediatricians no one noticed that she was still wearing her original tube. They just figured the surgeon would inform us when she needed a larger one. Common sense told me that after eight months of only breast milk and formula down this narrow tube, she needed more. When we called the hospital, they told us to add some cereal to thicken the milk and push it down with the plunger that came with the syringe. Now that was some feat. We really had to push it down hard, because the tube was so narrow. I knew Carla was not getting enough nutrition. She had been a regular plump baby, and now she was looking too thin for a baby her age.

Obviously, none of the homecare nurses were familiar with babies and G-tubes, because none of them said anything either. I decided to make an appointment with the surgeon who originally put Carla's tube in. She would know what to do. Bob took her down on one of my workdays. I came home that night eager to hear what had transpired in the visit.

"She said you can't put in a bigger one. This one is fine." I was incredulous.

"What do you mean she can't have a bigger one? Did you tell her she is losing weight?" I couldn't believe it. But this was the surgeon speaking. She was the authority.

We continued with the original G-tube. For a time I behaved like an obedient parent and accepted what the doctor said. But it gnawed at me. My concern did not diminish. Another month went by, and I was getting nervous. Carla just couldn't go on without nourishment. This was not right.

I discussed my concern with our new night nurse, Betty. She said, "Why don't you call another doctor? There is a neonatal intensive care unit in Pennsylvania where I live. I'll give you their number." I was impressed that Betty had come up with this novel idea. It simply hadn't occurred to me. But obviously, Carla's angels were working behind the scenes again, taking care of her.

I called the unit. The first call went directly through. I asked to speak to one of the neonatologists. Before I knew it, I was talking to the head doctor. He listened patiently to my dilemma. Then, not wanting to frighten me by the level of incompetence with which Carla had been handled, he assured me that Carla did need a bigger tube. He promised to give me the name of the doctor I should take her to. He was so kind; I knew from the tone of his voice that a big mistake had been made with Carla. He wished me the best, and I thanked him. The very next day we had an appointment with the new doctor. In a matter of minutes Carla had a bigger G-tube in place. Through this tube, we could pass a mixture of baby food and fluid to give her sufficient nutrition.

It was hard to forgive the doctor involved. I felt precious time had been lost. Carla remained very thin from that point on. There is no doubt she would have become seriously malnourished had her feeding tube not been replaced.

*　　*　　*

Not all was trauma with the G-tube. It did provide us with a funny incident—the one and only time when a crisis felt light. Every four hours we faithfully fed Carla. At the end of four hours, her stomach would be empty, ready for the next meal. At first, some of the nurses suggested checking her stomach to see if it was empty or not. After doing that for awhile it seemed obvious her stomach was empty. I wondered whether it was uncomfortable to have these juices sucked out of her stomach. There was no agreement among the nurses as to whether or not the procedure should be done.

Eventually, we figured out how much food she could digest, so we stopped checking. She had been digesting well for several weeks. So this morning, I prepared her usual amount of food and gathered all her feeding apparatus. Bob, in his ingenuity, had built a special device that we clamped the food syringe onto, and it worked well. The syringe was clamped to a board, freeing our hands for Carla. We always needed our hands free to suction, reposition, or push the food down a little bit with the plunger. Usually, the liquid food would just go down a few ccs by gravity. This time I watched for ten minutes as nothing went down.

"Okay," I thought. "I guess this food needs a little help. I got the plunger and pushed down a little. Nothing budged. I took the plunger out and held the syringe vertically above her belly to maximize the pull of gravity. The food wasn't budging. Normally it flowed easily. I began to get nervous. I felt sure something was very wrong.

I called down to the surgeon's office and reported the problem. They told me to come on down. Off we went, hoping for the best. When we arrived, one of the resident surgeons, a tall, thin, overworked-looking woman, listened to what we had to say and then examined Carla. Luckily, this young doctor was not one to rush to drastic conclusions.

The first thing she did was attach a syringe to Carla's tube and pull back on it. As she kept pulling, the syringe kept filling with stomach content. I watched in disbelief. Another syringe was attached, and another sixty ccs were taken out. She put it down, turned to me and said matter-of-factly, "Carla's stomach is completely full from her last meal. That is why nothing is going down."

She didn't add, "You idiot mother!" But I certainly felt like one. What a relief though! Another learning lesson. We wouldn't panic over this again. We were novices, but we were learning.

Chapter 13

Drawing Breath

A heavy pounding at my bedroom door roused me in the middle of the night.

"Help Mrs. Snyder! Carla has stopped breathing!" The nurse was screaming at my door. Instantly awake, charged with adrenaline, I ran into the living room. We both grabbed for the oxygen tank and applied the mask to Carla.

"Carla, don't leave. Don't die baby," I pleaded with her and commanded her.

She was lying so limp—too limp. I shook her back to breathing. Bob was by my side. We were all working together to bring her back. In a minute, she came around and took a breath. The nurse was still stunned. She explained that it happened suddenly. She only left the room for a minute to go into the kitchen to get her food. While she was gone, Carla caught her face in the pillow and could not turn her head. She was literally suffocating.

I just held Carla for a long time, thanking God for saving her. The incident awakened us to Carla's fragility. One minute she might be fine and the next, her breathing could stop. It wouldn't be the first time this scenario would occur. She would stop breathing many times. Luckily, we were there to rescue her each time. Some of the nurses would even take her into the bathroom with them. They were too afraid to leave her alone. Bob or I were always at her side when there was no nurse. Everything was so unpredictable with Carla. We always had to be on guard.

Every nurse who came through our door would have Carla's fragility drummed into them. Bob would provide explicit instructions on how to give her warm, nebulizing air treatments to keep her mucus thin. The nurses were schooled in the vital importance of suctioning her on a regular basis so that a mucus plug would not form to block her breathing. We came to know our daughter's body intimately. We knew what she needed to avoid running into problems. I would write explicit notes. In each of them, I added: "Be sure to tell Carla when you are going to suction her. Think about it—wouldn't you appreciate it if someone told you they were going to stick a tube down your nose?" Some nurses listened and some didn't.

There was one thing they always did remember to do...When in trouble, they yelled for help. Only a week had passed since the last incident, and my name was screamed in the middle of the night again. The nurse was lying next to Carla, totally freaked out. She had no idea what to do. I listened to her while taking a good look at Carla. By now I had learned to look at her first for clues as to what she needed. I grabbed the suctioning catheter. I sensed that she just had a plug stopping her breathing. I put the tube down her nose and watched it fill immediately with thick globs of mucus. As soon as I withdrew it, Carla took a breath. The same with the other nostril, gobs of mucus. She obviously had not been suctioned for hours. "Do you see all this mucus?" I wanted to yell at the nurse. "This is why we tell you to suction her regularly whether or not you think she needs it." That was the last night for that nurse.

It seemed that lately we were in for a string of one-night-stand nurses. Who were these people the nursing agency was sending over to us? Why did they send people who had no experience whatsoever with brain-injured babies? It was becoming clear they were sending anyone available to us. It was our job to train the nurses and determine their competence.

The next night we had a new nurse. Our daytime nurse, Joanne, said she knew this woman. She had graduated at the top of her class. We breathed a sigh of relief. Maybe we had a winner. In the middle of the night I woke up to a call for help.

"Mrs. Snyder!" Into the living room I ran. There was the nurse, panic stricken, holding the suction tube in her hand. "The alarm went off. She needs to be suctioned. What do I do?" What do you do? You suction her, you idiot! If my heart wasn't still pounding from the fear of being awakened, I would have laughed at the ridiculous scene. Suctioning Carla was as simple to us as changing her diaper. I showed her how to do what I assumed every nurse knew how to do.

"I don't think I can handle this job. It's too much responsibility." Good decision.

Some days I would be tired, going to work after these night escapades. My chiropractic work was a reprieve for me—a chance to immerse myself in other people's problems, rather than focusing on my own. Yet, it was hard to be away from Carla, even knowing that she was safe with Bob and our wonderful daytime nurse, Joanne.

Even at work, I would be interrupted by phone calls when there were problems with Carla. One mid-afternoon my husband called. "Carla is having trouble breathing. The fill-in nurse for Joanne has called the rescue squad. They are all here. Carla is on her way to the local emergency room. If the nurse had called the squad for help, I assumed it was serious. Without hesitation, I grabbed my coat while running out of the office yelling to my secretary to cancel the rest of the day's appointments. Like a maniac, I raced the twenty minutes to get from where I worked to our local hospital ER. In the car I prayed over and over. "Please Carla, please don't leave. Please God don't let me lose my baby."

As I pulled into the hospital parking lot, a van in front of me was moving so slowly. I laid into my horn, cursing his slowness. I didn't even know where the ER was. The man came over to me with a nasty look on his face, "What's your problem lady?"

"What's my problem? You asshole, my daughter is in the emergency room and you are slowing me down from getting there!" I screamed like a madwoman into his face. With that, he quickly got in his van and moved. I found the ER on the other side of the hospital, parked, and ran in praying, "Please God, don't let me find my daughter dead."

In the ER I located Carla, went to her side and said, "I'm here honey. Mommy is here right by your side." She was fine. She was breathing. They told me she had a major asthmatic attack and that it would be best if she was observed overnight in the hospital. That was fine with me. I was just so glad that she was okay. The crisis had passed.

*　　*　　*

What I didn't know immediately was that the nurse had not recognized Carla's incident as an asthma attack and had given Carla oxygen. Oxygen is not necessarily what you give a person who is having an asthma attack. I was uneasy with her assessment and treatment. I called the nurse and asked her, "Why did you give her oxygen?"

"I did for Carla what I would have done for my own child," she replied tersely. There was a moment when I wondered what to say next. "If you think I did something wrong, then I will never fill in for Carla again," she added. That took care of that.

This was our local hospital, and thankfully, it had a whole different feel to it. The pediatric floor was small, cheerful looking and only half-occupied. The staff was friendly and helpful. It was more like being in a hotel. Everything was presented and explained to me. There was a playroom at the end of the hall for Anora as well as a little kitchen where parents could make snacks. There was a pull-out bed within the chair in Carla's room, and I could even get one meal a day.

The atmosphere was so much more relaxed. It was a huge relief to be here after my other hospital experiences. Here the nurses could take time to be with Carla. I didn't have to worry about her being neglected. The medical staff was not rushed. I enjoyed meeting and talking with the nurses.

We settled into our routine. Every four hours Carla would get a nebulizing treatment with medication to help her breathing. The nurse would prepare it, and I would hold Carla in my lap and blow the mist over her nose.

By the middle of the night Carla was doing fine except for one problem. She was getting very hyper from the medication and could not sleep. Her oxygen numbers had been fine since the afternoon. Obviously, the intervals in between the medication needed to be changed. I asked the nurse for a Physician's Desk Reference so that I could read about the medication she was on. It mentioned hyperactivity as a side effect. It also explained that too much of the medication could actually have the reverse effect on the body. It could tighten up the bronchioles instead of opening them up. I knew again that Carla was getting too much of a drug. I asked the nurse, "Can we space these treatments further apart?"

"Only the doctor can change the order," she replied.

"Well, please get him on the phone for me," I said. "I need to speak to him about the dosage and how she is reacting."

I expected to have an adult conversation with a doctor who would respect my knowledge about Carla. What I got instead was the all too familiar I-am-the-doctor-and-know-best routine. This was one of the group pediatricians that I had not met. After a futile attempt at explaining to him what was happening, I hoped I would never have to see him person-to-person. He was so downright nasty on the phone. Maybe I had woken him up from too deep a sleep. I decided to take matters into my own hands. The next time her treatment was prepared and given to me, I would hold the tube mostly away from her nose.

In the morning she was pronounced well and we went home. It would be a few more weeks before another storm would burst.

Chapter 14

Soul Comfort

A knock on my bedroom at night. I have two thoughts at the same time; something is wrong, and it's not a crisis because no one is yelling or pounding at the door.

"I just wanted to let you know that Carla's temperature has been going up steadily and her oxygen rates aren't that great either, no matter what I do," Debbie told me in a concerned but calm voice.

I liked this new night nurse so much. I felt immediately a kind of easy, at-home feeling with her. She was a middle-aged black woman, short, and a little plump. She had two children of her own, and I knew she took good care of Carla. She had that same way of being lovingly attentive to Carla as Joanne did.

A few times, I woke up in the middle of the night to the sound of her singing a lullaby to Carla. Her lullabies sounded like those lovely black spirituals, and her voice was so deep and peaceful. Every time, I would smile and say, "Thank you, God, for this nurse." She stayed with us for a year. When she left, we never found another as good.

It was now 3 A.M. I picked Carla up and held her in my lap. She did not look well. "What's the matter sweetie?" I whispered to her. I suctioned her and noticed her secretions were thicker than normal.

"I'll call the doctor if you'd like and explain to him what's been happening," Debbie offered.

"Fine. Let's give a call."

The doctor decided we could wait until morning. At first light, Bob and I were waiting with Carla in the doctor's office. Dr. Ferraro was to see us. I was glad he was on today. He was a kind and good-natured doctor. We trusted him. He examined Carla and looked at us. I knew from his face it was not good news.

"It's pneumonia again," he said. "She will need to be hospitalized." I knew he was going to say that. My whole body felt heavy at the thought of being in the hospital again…of Carla having pneumonia again. "She will be able to stay at this hospital to be treated, however." That was the good news. I tried to feel grateful that at least she would be nearby, in a hospital where I didn't have to fight for everything. Carla and I went upstairs while my husband went home to get my overnight things. By now, he knew everything that needed to go in my bag. It had unfortunately become a routine.

We were in the same room again. This time oxygen was pumped into a big plastic tent set up around Carla, and she was given medications. I could reach under the tent to touch her and cover her. It turned cold and clammy in her little tent. I was glad I was there to change her clothes, which quickly got damp from the cool mist. "Carla, Carla, I'm sorry we have to be here again, but you'll get better sweetie. I know you will." I murmured to her encouragingly.

Later that day, my husband and Anora came to visit. The only one who ever had a good time in the hospital was Anora. She especially liked the kitchen where the goodies were. It seemed there was always a leftover ice cream in the freezer or a soda on the shelf. These were treats she didn't typically have at home, so the hospital was okay with her.

The next day Carla started to make a dramatic improvement. I could tell how well she was doing from the doctor's tone of voice. It had changed from serious to light. The medical staff was surprised at how quickly she was recovering. But that's how Carla did it. As quickly as she got sick, she would get better.

On the fourth day I started a conversation with the doctor, inquiring when was the soonest that we could go home. He was understanding about my feelings and said he would release her as soon as possible. He knew by now that we could handle Carla competently. The next day, he told us we could leave. Carla would go home with one liter of oxygen by way of a nasal canula, a piece of plastic that wrapped around her head with holes placed by her nostril to deliver oxygen.

"We're out of here Carla," I told her one more time, tired but happy. "You did it again honey. You got better, and now we can go home." Home for a brief respite and for a change of pace. Time for something of peace to enter our lives.

* * *

It was summertime, a warm welcome summer after a tough winter of trials with Carla. For several weeks now she was doing great. During the day I would picnic outside in our lovely backyard with Carla and Anora. Under a tree we would lay amongst pillows and books and food and drink.

Anora and I would take Carla's clothes off so she could get some full sun. When we had her on her stomach we would tell Carla, "We're sunning your buns, Carla!" It seemed to be just fine with her.

When it was really hot I would give her baths in her baby tub on the patio. We would call that her swimming pool. Carla still didn't have any facial expressions or make any sounds. The only way I would know she didn't like something was if her body stiffened up. That meant she was afraid. That happened the very first time I gave her a bath in our bathtub. What I thought would be so relaxing for her was frightening. I guess we had bathed her on towels on the floor for so long that this new experience was just too different. I'm sure she was also picking up on my anxiety. You had to be careful giving Carla a bath. Because she could not swallow, no water could enter her mouth. The first time, I probably held her too tightly. She stiffened up so much for me that I was afraid I was not going to be able to hold her. That was a quick bath. The next time, she relaxed. Gradually she became accustomed to her nightly routine. And gradually I found that I could give her a bath and not have to worry about drowning her.

Laura, a healer friend of mine called and invited me to come to New York City. A holy woman from India was going to be at a church and she thought it would be great for Carla to come and be blessed by this woman. My initial reaction was tainted by prejudice. Who is this woman from another country, and who says she is holy? I thanked her for the invitation and told her I would think about it.

The next morning, Sunday, I woke up with a change of mind and decided in a moment that I would go. This was no easy task. I had Carla and her portable suction device and all her feeding equipment to pack, as well as Anora and my stepdaughter, Taryn. Miraculously, it all got done easily, and we were on our way.

I wasn't exactly sure where the church was. It was way uptown along the river, and I figured I would just find it one way or another. We did get lost, but I stopped and asked a woman where the street was. She gave me great directions and ten minutes later we were parking outside the church. It was a very old church. It must have been beautiful in its day, and it still had a grand and stately feel to it. We walked through the dark, cool corridors to the elevator and continued upstairs, where this woman named Amma was conducting a service and blessing.

I was hot, a little tense from having been temporarily lost, and unsure of what I was doing here. The moment I entered the room where Amma was seated, all my discomfort vanished. In an instant my senses were flooded. It was awe-inspiring. In the back of the room beautiful music from instruments I could not even name wafted towards me, and an exquisitely cool breeze brushed my arms from the open windows behind us. There was a delightful fragrance of incense. In the middle of the room a peaceful woman sat, all in white, with a blissful smile on her face. This experience was so different from anything I had ever known—the music, the many people dressed in white, this woman who would hug people to her bosom, murmur words consolingly in Indian and then shower you with petals and give you little chocolates.

After we had received our hug and blessing I sat with Carla for hours alongside the wall of the room. I became very aware of how relaxed Carla was. She took a nap in my arms for a long time without needing to be suctioned. My whole body relaxed with her as I just sat and took in the peaceful environment. After a while, I took her to a small adjoining room to feed her. I felt no awkwardness feeding her through the G-tube around these people. A few of them came up and acknowledged what a special baby Carla was. Finally it was time to go home. I was grateful for the whole day and thanked God for opening my heart to this experience.

This was another step towards a restful place where I would experience and devote myself to learning more about God. The first step had been a local metaphysical type of Christian Church. There, I had begun to explore being part of a spiritual group searching for answers and committed to spiritual values. As much as I liked this church, they only had one service, and it always conflicted with Carla's care schedule. "Okay," I thought, "It is time to find another church. Maybe there is a reason for this change." Many times I had passed a beautiful old church on the main street of Clinton. I picked this church because it was convenient, and I liked the way it looked. I thought those were the only reasons.

The next Sunday I decided to attend service by myself. I was a little nervous. I knew no one and I hadn't attended a mainstream Christian church since my childhood. I walked hesitantly into the back. This day everyone happened to be crammed into the fellowship hall due to repairs in the main sanctuary. A man noticed my hesitation. He came over immediately to welcome me with a warm smile and give me a church bulletin for the day. I settled into the service. The minister and congregation were not nearly as stiff as I imagined; I relaxed. Midway through the service the minister announced that today, a baby girl would be baptized. I thought nothing of it. As the proud parents brought forward their beautiful little girl in her white christening gown my heart suddenly sank. The contrast between this child and Carla hit me like a bolt. This child was so healthy and happy. She had a good life ahead of her. Here were her parents, who had no reason to expect anything less.

And my baby? I didn't even want to bring her out in public. I didn't want to chance people's pity or rejection. The tears were coming up uncontrollably. I looked around to see how I could get up and leave quietly. I slipped out of the back door into the hallway. The same man who had greeted me was watching. I could feel his concern for me as I walked out.

"It's too hard God," I cried outside the doors. "It's too hard to see. Won't my baby ever be well, won't she ever be healed?" I thought of those words I had felt so long ago: everything was going to be okay. I wondered, "But when God? When will she be well and how?" I resolved not to give up, but to keep searching for someone to help Carla. There had to be someone, there just had to be.

Chapter 15

The Academy

"There is a holistic medical doctor I've heard of that you might want to try," a friend mentioned in passing one day. "He works a lot with vitamins and herbals." Click went my brain. Let's try him.

The next week we were in his office. We had been warned about the endless waiting time, so we booked an appointment early in the morning. Finally, it was our turn and we were shown into the exam room. His office was in the bottom of his old Victorian house, so it had a different feel to it. The dark wood of the floors and the walls were unlike any doctor's office I had ever been in; the atmosphere was not as sterile.

In walked Dr. Carr, a tall, thin black man. He had on casual clothes under the typical white doctor's coat. He exuded calmness and an "I am not in a hurry" attitude about him. From the unhurried time he spent with us I could easily see how he got very behind schedule.

His initial exam was very thorough, and I liked the fact that he took his time and talked a lot about Carla in a positive way. He was the first doctor who spoke of any possibility of Carla's improvement. For some reason he went off on a tangent, talking about his own questions regarding brain-injured children and what could be done for them. Casually he said, "Do you know there is a special academy for brain-injured children in Philadelphia?" When he mentioned the name of the place I sat there, stunned.

I knew exactly which school he was speaking about. It was a place many of my chiropractic friends had taken their healthy children to advance their reading, math, and music skills, all at an early age. I had formed an unfavorable opinion because I considered it the kind of place parents would take their kids so they could brag about how smart their children were...I never knew they also had an extensive program for brain-injured children. How ironic. What I had rejected was now something I felt hopeful about.

I sat there, letting this new information seep in...this academy was so nearby, and I hadn't even known it. It was the first piece of positive information I had received in a while and was I excited! As soon as we got home, I called the place, found out when the next week-long program for parents was scheduled, and signed us up for it.

I went to the library and found the book written by the founder of the Academy. It was so fascinating I could hardly put it down. All his pioneering work had been done with cerebral palsied children. The results had been so good that he had gone on to work with healthy children. As I read of case histories and all their accomplishments, I felt hope for Carla rising in me.

I started doing one of the exercises for vision immediately. I had to shine a bright light in Carla's pupils in a completely darkened room many times a day. The purpose of the exercise was to stimulate the pupilary response. I became enthusiastic when I read in their literature of blind children who could now see because of these exercises.

On our next visit, I couldn't wait to tell our local pediatrician the good news about this special academy I'd found. He was a very conservative, grandfatherly type. I could tell immediately from the look on his face that he did not share my excitement at all. "But, doctor," I gushed, "isn't it incredible—the results they have had with such children as Carla?" There was no response. It was obvious his mind was sealed shut on this issue.

His reaction baffled me. I could not comprehend how a doctor interested in the welfare of children could be so negative. I spoke excitedly about this academy, but he was definitely not thrilled, or even interested.

His view of the situation was so far removed from my own. I could never get used to it.

To me, the human body was full of infinite possibility for healing. The body was a miracle. I had seen enough in my own healing practice to know the experts weren't always right. Often it was just a matter of putting the right pieces together for that person. My hope was animated by the chiropractic philosophy of my body's intelligence fully incorporated into my whole being, always seeking perfect health. This belief was part of what kept me constantly looking and constantly optimistic—more so than many others. The vitalistic philosophy of chiropractic was one of the main drawing factors for me to become a chiropractor. And the approach to using natural remedies along with adjustments instead of harsh chemical drugs was the other factor.

I remembered the first time I had met a chiropractic student at the age of 25. I listened in amazement as he explained what he was learning in chiropractic school. I had been searching for a different route to go in the health field. I had been a medical lab technician for several years and wanted to move up but didn't know exactly to where or to what. I had been looking at the whole array of professions including nursing, pharmaceutical practice, eye care. No one had ever mentioned chiropractic. All I knew of it was that once a chiropractor had helped my brother with a knee problem. As he spoke, I knew this was what I wanted—a profession where I could help people get well naturally. I made up my mind at the end of our conversation. There wasn't a question as to what else I would do. It was a done deal.

The more I read about the Academy and all the different types of experts they had on staff, the more I became convinced this was the place. They had the answers.

Finally, the big week arrived. We had decided we would drive back and forth for the week. They would be long days, but I was so looking forward to it. We found the place easily enough. It was located in a nice neighborhood of Philly. The location was a former estate that had been donated to the academy. It was so Philadelphia—all brick, stately looking, and surrounded by beautiful pine trees. Two new buildings had been added: the auditorium where we had our lectures, and the adjacent building where the children were examined and the rehabilitation programs given. Meals were served in the mansion.

We walked into the modern amphitheater. It was freezing cold. We found out later they had a reason for that, too. It kept exhausted parents awake during lectures. I didn't think any of us would have fallen asleep, though. We were there to learn how to help our kids get better. Most of us kept rapt attention all day long to what was being said.

In front of each chair were the parents' names and places of origin. It was amazing to see places like Greece, Spain, Mexico, Japan, and England listed. Parents had come literally from all over the world for this week. They had headphones so they could listen to the translated lectures.

It felt so good to be with parents who were in the same situation. We talked with so many others and heard our own frustrations echoed in their experiences. We weren't the only ones who had to deal with so much. It felt right to be with other parents who weren't willing to give up on their kids either, who were willing to do whatever was needed to help their kids get well.

The founder of the Academy finished the first day with a short anecdote. He was being interviewed by a reporter who asked him how he could in all fairness dare to give parents of brain-injured children the hope that they might get better. The founder was astounded by her question. He told her that of all things hope is what parents need most. Hope got a parent out of bed in the morning to do all that was necessary for his or her child. It offered a parent the vision of a better future. How cruel it would be to deny that! Without hope, there would only be despair and a "Why bother at all?" attitude. Of course it was right to give parents hope. I couldn't have agreed with him more.

The third day we were shown how to evaluate the extent of our child's brain injury and determine the location of the damage in the brain. They had devised an impressive system of doing this. As we went down the chart, filling out the information, my heart began to sink. Carla was way down on the chart. There were categories for mild, moderate, severe, and profoundly brain-injured children. Carla fell into this last category. There was only one more extreme category: coma. I wanted to cry from the hopelessness of her condition. I looked at my husband. He read my thoughts. "Just because she is at the bottom doesn't mean there isn't hope," he said reassuringly. It was all I needed to hear. I would keep my mind focused on this one possibility.

The fourth day we were given the option to have Carla evaluated. We had already decided we would, as had most of the other parents. The next day, we brought Carla down. All the parents and kids waited in one big room while we were called to each different specialist. I had the chance to see kids that my heart went out to. They seemed so much worse off than Carla. One young Japanese girl lay on her belly. The only part of her that she could move was her head. She was so thin I couldn't help but wonder how she could stay alive.

Several people carried a teenage boy in. He had been in a car accident and could move no part of his body from the neck down. There were several Downs Syndrome children, a lot of cerebral palsied children, and amongst all of these, a couple of kids who could run around and make noises. They seemed so normal compared to everyone else, I wondered what their problem could possibly be.

Finally it was our turn. Our first evaluation would be for tactile competence. The instructor explained she would be poking Carla with some sharp devices to see her reaction. I listened carefully to what she was going to do. As she approached us I said to Carla, "Carla, a lady is going to poke you in a couple of different places on your body. She needs to figure out what your reaction will be." She waited until I was finished talking to Carla. We watched as Carla made very little notice of scratchy paper on her skin, of tiny little pin pricks on her hands. She made no effort to withdraw her hands.

After several minutes of testing the woman said, "Okay. Now I will take you to your next evaluation, which will be for auditory competence." As she walked us into the room next door, she introduced us and turned to leave. "Oh, and this is a special mother," she said smiling at me, "She explains everything to her daughter." I was taken aback. Someone had actually acknowledged my way of speaking to Carla as positive instead of a waste of time. My heart filled with gratitude towards her for noticing.

This person made loud noises next to Carla's ears, laid her down on a device that flashed a bright light and emitted a loud noise at the same time. My husband and I jumped at the noise. Carla barely had a reaction.

We continued to have her visual competence checked, the size of her chest measured, and lastly, a mobility challenge. Carla was placed at the top of a sliding board of sorts, a piece of wood covered with leather at a slight incline. The idea behind this was ingenious. With any attempt of even lifting the head or moving the arms the child would move forward due to the incline. This would motivate continued movement and introduce the sensation of movement forward. We cheered Carla on at the bottom. She made a few attempts to move forward.

Finally our long day was over. It was a fascinating day, watching everyone intently evaluate Carla. I was so impressed with the dedication of the staff and the upbeat attitudes. The atmosphere was one of unlimited possibility.

The next day, we returned with Carla to be given our program of at-home treatment. To this academy, all things were possible for brain-injured children with the cooperation and hard work of the parents. To them parents were the solution to helping get sick kids well.

Our primary goal was to improve Carla's health—her respiratory status. My husband and I knew this was key to her survival. The first part of the program shown to us was the respiratory masking program. Its purpose was to rapidly increase delivery of oxygen to the brain and also, to increase the rate and depth of breathing. It was exactly what Carla needed. Her chest was small due to the lack of sufficient deep breathing. Fifty times a day we would place a little plastic mask over her nose for forty seconds.

We were shown how to make these masks and how to fit one securely over her nose. We could immediately see how she was forced to take deep breaths. It also served another purpose. It helped bring secretions up. Carla's chronological age at this point was eleven and a half months. Her neurological age was assessed to be two and a half months.

Next came her visual program. Her diagnosis included an inadequate light reflex bilaterally, and no ability to see outlines bilaterally. Thirty times a day we would take her into a dark room and shine a bright light for one second in the right eye, one second in the left for a total of a minute. Then we would slowly move the light on the wall for a minute, encouraging her to follow its direction. In addition, we would show her black and white slides ten times a day, hold her in our lap, and identify each picture aloud.

Her auditory program had three parts. To improve her startle reflex, we would bang wooden blocks thirty times a day. To create a vital response to threatening noise, we would blow an air horn thirty times. And to foster her ability to hear meaningful sounds, we used different musical instruments thirty times a day, telling her what each sound was. All these efforts aimed to improve her diagnoses of insufficient startle reflex and non-vital response to threatening sounds.

To create ability to understand two words or more we would talk loudly and clearly, and orient her at all times. That was something we had already been doing.

Her tactile program had two parts also. To create vital sensation we would brush her entire body with a firm brush, twenty times a day. To create gnostic sensation we would use contrasting sensation, silk and sand paper on her body twenty times a day. We hoped this exercise would help improve her ability to perceive pain bilaterally and her appreciation of light touch. This exercise was also intended to address the fact that Carla had no sterognosis, or sensory discrimination, on the left side. Carla could not distinguish a coin from a cotton ball, or a cotton ball from a pin. She also had a persistent Babinski reflex. The Babinski reflex is a newborn reflex, normal up to the age of two. To detect it, the bottom of the foot is stroked with a moderately sharp object stroke from the bottom to the ball of the foot. The toes flex with the sensation.

For mobility, we would have to make our own incline plane and put her on it seventy times a day. The goal was to have her go all the way down and crawl the length of her head at the bottom. We would also be doing something called patterning, which involved three people. We would lay her belly-down on a table. The person at the head of the table would move her head from side to side, while each person at the side would move her arms and legs up at a right angle. This was to be done for five minutes, twelve times a day. Her evaluation revealed the ability to move her arms and legs, but not very well, and she was unable to crawl. In manual competence, her evaluation report noted a bilateral grasp reflex, but no vital release on either side of the body.

To stimulate her light reflex and vital response simultaneously, we had to make the same device she had been placed on in her evaluation. We would place her on the startle box. Underneath, a bright light would flash and a loud noise would go off at the same time.

In addition we would put blinking X-mas lights along her incline plane and black and white patterns wherever possible.

I looked at all we were to do in bewilderment and wondered how we would do it all in a day, each day. Besides the program, she still had to be fed, bathed, suctioned and chest-percussed all day. But I was determined. If that was what they wanted us to do, then I would sure do it.

As Bob busied himself buying all the supplies to make her incline plane and startle device, I plunged into the rest of her routine. As soon as she finished breakfast, we would start.

First, I would put the plastic mask on her face and suction her a bit. Then, off we went, to our only completely dark room, at the back of the house in order to shine the flashlight in her eyes. From there, back to the foyer to show her slides, then back, to lay her down, bang noises in her ears, and rub her body with soft and hard fabrics. Then I'd blow the air horn. Then, play a musical instrument. Next, I'd place Carla on the incline board to encourage her to come down the slide. I'd call for my husband and Anora to come help do a pattern on the table. Then, she had to be suctioned. Her back had to be thumped a little. And then it was time to repeat the whole scenario over again. Again and again, all day long. Rush rush rush. Try to do everything as many times as they had told us to do it.

After three days, I was a complete wreck. I sat down on the floor with Carla, and sobbed, "I can't do this. It's too much." No matter how organized I was, there was no way I could possibly do all that they had recommended in a day. It was impossible. Worst of all, Carla reacted to my tension and sense of rushing by stiffening up more than usual. I knew she was not having a good time either. I had to call our advisor at the Academy. I said to my husband, "Maybe they will have a suggestion…" I called the advisor and told her how impossible it was to do everything. I explained that I didn't even have time to snuggle and hold Carla for a minute. She listened sympathetically.

"Well that's not good. You don't have a minute to hug her. It's probably too much program work. Do as much as you can." Too much program? If they knew it was too much of a program, why did they ever give us that much in the first place? My mind wondered about that, but I quickly pushed it aside. I had to get back to work. I was convinced this was the ticket to save Carla, and I was going to give it my best.

In a week my husband had the incline plane and startle box (as we called it) all finished. It was expertly done with every attention to detail. This was for Carla and it had to be the best. I was sure no other baby had equipment as nice as Carla's. Meanwhile all our family had been trained to help with patterning. It was a joke around our house that anyone who came to the door would be trained on the spot if we happened to need them. Patterning was that important.

The only problem with patterning was that it could only be done at certain times. Sufficient time had to elapse after a feeding to avoid any reflux. Anora, who was five now, was trained to help, as well as my eight-year-old step-granddaughter, Ashley. Patterning did afford us five minutes of sitting though, and that reprieve was always welcome. It also afforded us five minutes of time for conversation—another bonus.

On this particular Saturday, I was doing a pattern with Ashley and Anora. I turned Carla's head from side to side while Anora and Ashley patiently pushed her arms and legs. Their sweet little faces and their willingness to help Carla struck me. How blessed I was to have their help! How right it was for them to learn the lesson of giving to someone else…

While I was at the pattern table, Edna was up to some of her tricks. She was telling Lisa, my stepdaughter (Ashley's mom), and her boyfriend, Marc, about all the equipment that had to be made for Carla.

"Oh Marc, perhaps you would like to see how her light and sound box works," she said so innocently. From the tone of her voice I had a suspicion he was going to be in for some trouble. She led Marc to the back room. "Now just put your head here on the top of it and I will show you how it works," she said. Marc obligingly did so. The next second, she flipped the switch, and poor Marc had a little startle reaction of his own. He nearly jumped a foot off the box. I swear that all his dark hair as well as his mustache stood on end for at least a split second.

"Well Marc, I guess there is nothing wrong with your startle reflex," Edna said.

But Edna would be getting her comeuppance soon enough.

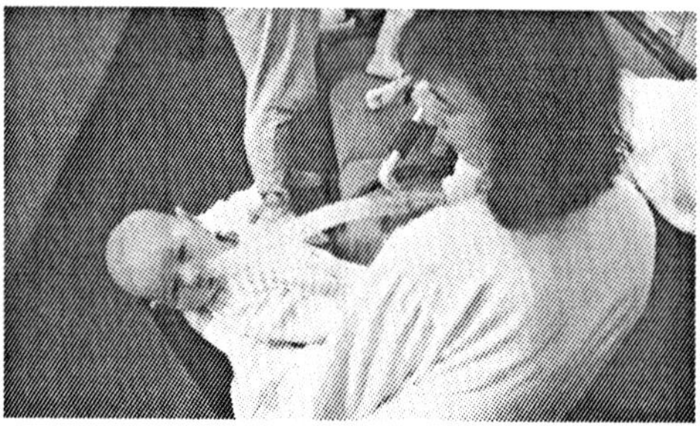

Mom giving Carla a warm, moist nebulizing treatment to keep Carla's secretions loose

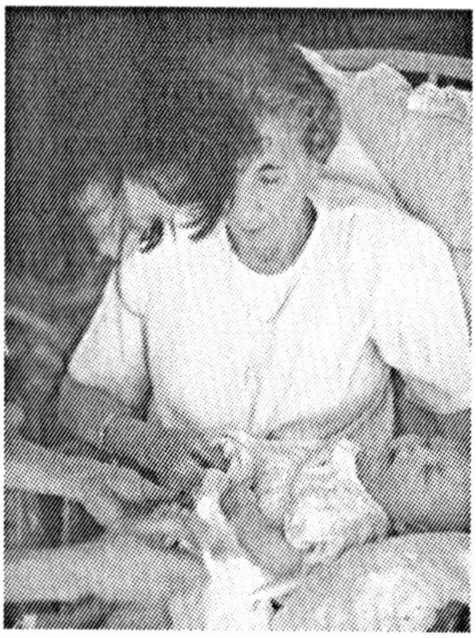

Mom checking Carla's G-tube while Grandmother, Claire, holds Carla

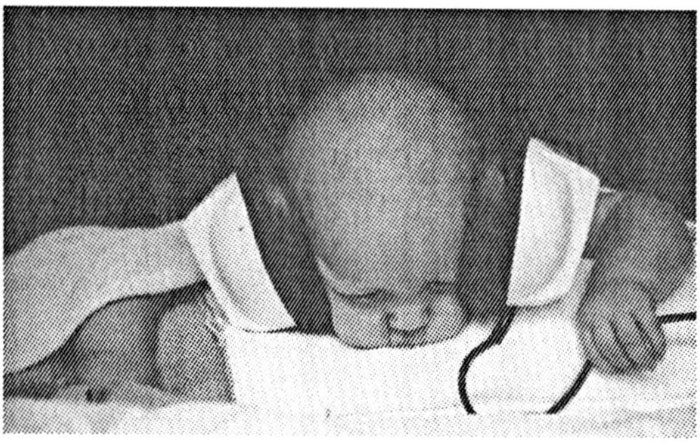

Carla listening to one of her favorite pieces, Beethoven's 9th

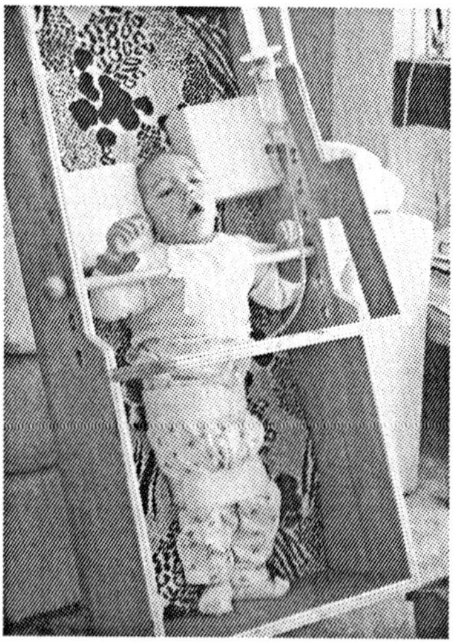

Carla at eighteen months in her new special standup device. A plastic feeding tube is inserted into her stomach for feeding.

Chapter 16

The G-Tube Caper

This chapter was written by Edna Doll

There's something about my niece, Cindy—a kind of magic hard to define. If she says, "Jump!" I ask the proverbial, "How high?" If she says five feet, I jump five feet. "Impossible," you say. Of course, it is, but I do it because she says so. Never mind my arthritis. Somehow I'm able to do it. That's where the magic comes in.

It always has been that way, and then, of course, when Carla came along it became a much bigger game. "Go to the drug store and get so and so," Cindy would say, and I'd head off immediately. Small matter that I didn't even know where the drug store was. I'd hone right in. Same thing with the health food store. I always found the most expedient route. It never failed.

"Make soup out of those marrow bones and vegetables." Cindy would say. There I'd be, cutting up stuff, tossing bowls and pots around and guess what? It would be delicious. Amazing! I would just go ahead and do anything she said—cook, bake, put the baby on the sliding board, take her for her eye exercises, purée, iron, count out, change the diaper, make juice, weigh, measure, aid in patterning, liquefy, shred, WHATEVER! Naturally, I'd never let Cindy know I didn't know how, couldn't do that, or was highly confused. Never! I'd rather have died than to let Cindy down.

But one day was almost my undoing.

"I'll tell you what," said Cindy. "There's that whole pile of toys in the garage that we need to get rid of. Today's the day we can do it since Bob is off playing golf. If he were here he'd be lugging the stuff back in as fast as we'd be lugging it out. So now's our chance. We can load up the van."

"Where we taking it?" I put in.

"There's a little church not far from here," explained Cindy. "They're looking for things for a rummage sale. We can drive right over."

With her usual efficiency, Cindy packed the back of the van. Then, she bundled Carla in her pink snowsuit and fastened her securely in her car seat. Disappearing into the house one more time, she emerged with a covered jar of Carla's food. Now came the clincher! "You can sit in back with the baby and feed her as we go along," she said, handing me the jar.

Feed her as we go? Who, me? I looked around, but nobody else was there. Yikes! Phew! One didn't take feeding Carla lightly. It took diligent attention to detail—and now—in a moving vehicle??

"Ah, ah—" words kept zipping through my mind. Never say no, never say can't—me? ME: Oh sure. Why not? No problem. Oh no—not much. But if Cindy said I could—well then—of course. Piece of cake. Oh yeah! That magic better work! Even so, I was scared.

We took off. My niece Cindy, is no slouch as a driver. We zoomed along those country roads and around the curves without losing much time. Because I was too short to sit in the seat and reach over to feed Carla, I perched precariously on the armrest, keeping my body balanced like the skier I once was. "Look Ma! No hands!" I uncovered the jar of warm food. It was made of puréed avocado and organic vegetables formulated by Cindy herself, who was determined that Carla should have the healthiest diet possible. It was of a runny consistency and an awful green. But color didn't matter to Carla. She was not an ordinary baby into whose mouth you just popped a bottle, Instead, she had a tube that went directly into her small stomach.

The tube had to be opened and please, please don't lose its tiny plug—the tube had to be connected to a glass vial marked with centimeters, so please, please pour the right amount and please, please, DON'T SPILL, and with your THIRD hand, wrap the extra food so the temperature stays even, and with your OTHER hand, adjust the tube so the food moves steadily into Carla's tummy; please, please, NOT TOO FAST to cause pains, and please, please, NOT TOO SLOW or it will get stuck, and above all, please, please, don't have to use the plunger to unstick it and WHERE is this church anyway, we must have gone eight hundred miles by now; so please, please, let us get there, and please, please, don't let me fall on Carla and squish her as we go round the bend, and please, please don't let me slip completely off this perch and land splattering on the floor, and please, please, let me get it all right—!

And what do you know—I did get it all right! The magic worked!! I didn't squish Carla or fall on the floor. That sweet baby took the food smoothly and looked absolutely adorable in her little pink snowsuit. I was so grateful, I changed my litany of please-pleases to oh-thank-you-thank-yous as we swung into the parking area of the church.

Just as we got there, and with newly acquired confidence, I poured the last of the food into the vial and gave it a most careful little nudge with the plunger and Oh wow! What happened!! There was a wild eruption of dark runny avocado! Like green lava, it spread over everything—Carla's chin, her tiny fingers, the car seat; a good-sized blob even slid down the sleeve of my jacket! What a mess! Panic! I must have turned as green as the mix.

Luckily, Cindy didn't look at us as she got out of the van. She headed directly into the church with an armload of toys saying, "I'll be right back."

Feeling like a total wreck, I went immediately into my litany of please-pleases again as I reached for the box of Kleenex and paper towels, which I knew Bob always kept in the car. "Please, please don't let Cindy see this awful mess," I moaned as I frantically wiped off Carla's sweet face and ten fingers. Please, please don't let the snowsuit stain; please, please help me get the goo out of the intricacies of the car seat; please, please help me get this all cleaned up—.

The stuff was gloppy and pervasive and the blob in my sleeve kept rolling around and seeping out in squishy dribbles. Small matter. Never mind me, just get the rest cleaned up. A huge pile of stained Kleenex and paper towels was piling up as I tossed the debris on the floor behind me.

I was preoccupied, madly wiping up, but glancing at the church, I saw the door opening! Out came Cindy with three friends in tow to help with the toys and see the baby! I was horrified! My fingers flew even faster as the foursome came closer and closer. Fortunately, they had to travel a little distance. Just before Cindy opened the door, I chucked the last Kleenex over my shoulder and there we sat, Carla and I, as pristine and neat as if nothing had ever happened. Carla, bless her heart, was sleeping peacefully. Everyone admired that sweet little angel and didn't pay much attention to me. Good thing, too. I was completely freaked out.

"Well, that's a good job done," said Cindy on the way home, "and I'm glad Carla had her lunch."

"Me too," I murmured earnestly. I had moved off the armrest and was sitting luxuriously in the seat, watching the trees go by as my hyperventilation quieted down.

Back at the house, Cindy took care of Carla while I surreptitiously dumped the whole load of Kleenexes and paper towels into my trunk. "Let sleeping dogs lie," I thought to myself. "You needn't tell Cindy what happened." But I said to her over a cup of tea, "You owe me for that outing."

"I do?" she asked, "Why?"

"Well, you know it wasn't easy," I replied in what was the understatement of the year.

"Nothing to it," said Cindy, "I knew you'd be able to handle it just fine." And she gave me one of her sweetest smiles.

*   *   *

I could hardly wait to get home. Immediately, I phoned Claire, my sister-in-law, Cindy's mother. "Listen," I said, "If ever Cindy wants you to go someplace in the van and asks you to feed the baby on the way, just say NO! Got it? Just say NO!" And I hung up. It was going to take me several double-dipped chocolate ice cream cones over several days to get over that trip.

Chapter 17

The Rigors of Devotion

In a few short months we had settled into our new routine. The Academy had warned us that our lives would not be the same. It was drilled into us that we were never to take a day off from doing the program. And they explicitly stated that with the exception of patterning, only the parents were to do the program. They told us our social lives would be reduced to zero.

I really had no problem with giving up ordinary things like going to lunch with a friend, or out to dinner or the movies. I had one focus, and that was to get Carla well. We always had someone over our house anyway, family or friends to help us pattern so I didn't feel I was deprived. Everyone now came to my house to "play" with Carla. The days that Carla felt well, we actually had fun, and once I got over my initial craziness, Carla relaxed and never made any signs that she didn't like what we were doing. The only thing she clearly did not like was being suctioned. Many a time when I approached her with the suction tube she would make a spastic swipe at it with her arm. At those times, I wondered if it was just a spastic reaction, or rather a statement on her part: "Get that damn thing away from me". I would always tell her, "I don't want to have to do it either Carla, but you know we have to." She was really such a trooper, letting us whisk her from one activity to the next, letting us suction her and thump her. She took it all graciously.

Even though I had relaxed a bit with the program, I was still known as the drill sergeant, making sure everything was done on time. I lived by the clock. When it was a minute before the patterning, I would call out to everyone, "Time for a pattern!" Whether it was a call to the basement for my husband or to the kitchen for my mother or Edna, or to the living room for the nurse, they all knew that when I yelled, "Pattern!" they had better get their butts into the hallway in position ready to go. I didn't realize how regimented I was with this until one morning when Edna was helping us out. It was one minute to "go" and I yelled out, "Pattern!" in my customary way. To my amazement, my aunt came out of the bathroom—not walking, but running. Knowing how adamant I was about being on time, she hadn't properly fastened her pants. She came running out half-undressed, pants unzipped, underwear exposed. It was the funniest sight. I just cracked up. I reminded myself, "Lighten up. Don't make people crazy around you. And definitely allow time for everyone to go to the bathroom."

Of course, we didn't do the program like robots. We talked constantly to Carla. We encouraged and applauded her all day. Carla would have some good days when she would not only get all the way down the incline plane, but also manage to crawl a little at the end. Then I would pick her up, hold her high in the air, and say "Yes, you are our 'can-do' Carla and you are doing it!" In between running from one place to another in the house, I would be kissing her.

Edna said one day, "Do you realize how much you smooch that baby!" Probably not. I only knew I loved her so much, my lips on her cheeks were just an expression of that love.

*　　　*　　　*

It was the first reevaluation at the academy for Carla. Six months had gone by. We would again go to two days of lecture, and she would be reevaluated and given a new program. I was really pleased at the progress I felt she had made. She was definitely doing more crawling on the incline board. There was also a definite change in her pupilary response. When I shone the light in her pupils, there was a well-defined constriction. I knew this didn't mean she could see, but it was an improvement. Also, from doing all the masking, her breathing was much better; her little chest that was so sunken and small was larger, not as concave as it had been.

Sitting in classes at the Academy again, I was so thrilled. For the first time in a year I truly felt hopeful. I felt that we had found The Place. At the end of the day, my husband commented with gruff sarcasm, "They could really make these lectures shorter. The lecturer is too long-winded." I dismissed his comment as a natural aversion to sitting for long periods of time, although part of me agreed. I was too focused on the experience of being back in a roomful of parents all in the same boat, talking and sharing during the breaks.

The third day, we brought Carla down for her reevaluation. I was a little nervous because we had broken one of the golden rules about not having anyone but the parents do the program outside of the patterning. Our daytime nurse helped us out quite a bit the days I worked. The threat over our heads was removal from the program for infractions of the rules, and of course, there was no way I was going to take a chance with that.

We sat down for our first six-month interview. I had a panicked flash thought: "Oh God, does Bob remember The Rule about parents only doing the program and absolutely no one else helping?" My heart started to pound a little quicker when I realized I hadn't gone over the correct answers to give on this interview.

The staff person began, "So tell me how has it been going? How have you been managing to do all the program?" Before I could say anything, Bob started, "Well you know, it has been really hard to do all the program and take care of our other daughter and take care of the house, but it's been a little easier now that we trained our daytime nurse." I wanted to sink under the table. My nightmare was happening. I gave him a hard kick under the table, but it was too late. The damage was done.

The staff person visibly stiffened and said in that strict authoritative tone, "You ARE aware ONLY the parents are allowed to do the program, correct?"

"Oh yes," I interjected, beaming my brightest smile, and stopping Bob from saying anything else. "What my husband means is she has been trained to do all the medical things we have to do for Carla, and that gives us more time to do the program." I don't remember what else I said, but I got us out of it somehow.

When we left the room, I hissed at Bob, "Don't you remember The Rule...the one they drummed into us about ONLY parents doing the program?"

"Yeah, but I thought they would be a little more understanding of our situation," he answered, obviously annoyed at their response. He felt bad that he screwed up and was equally annoyed at their insistence about the rule. I was just so afraid of being kicked out, so horribly afraid of losing what I saw as the only chance to help Carla live in and heal her body.

During the break we talked to other parents. Talking to them soothed us greatly. We told a couple how we had screwed up that morning. The mom replied, "Oh please! I guess I better not tell them I take every Sunday off. Every Sunday we all just get in the car and go away for a change of pace. After doing the program all week, I need a day off." I started to take note of how much more relaxed the parents who took a little time off were. Those who wouldn't had the fear drummed into them that every moment not spent on the program doomed their child to failure, and that the Academy would find out and kick them out of the program.

We returned Carla to each area to be reviewed by the same people that originally tested her. They asked us what type of progress we thought she had made. We said fair. They noted poor progress in their notes with a slight quantitative gain. She was now nineteen months old and assessed neurologically at two. Eight months; obviously not much of a gain over the past six months. Besides her chest growth, the only area in which she showed appreciable changes were her vital response to threatening sounds. After we had tubes inserted in her ears to drain the fluid, she responded quite well to the air horn. She made a loud *whooing* sound to it. We realized then, that the fluid in her ears had prevented her from hearing. There had been no big changes, so her basic program would remain the same.

Later, all the parents and staff gathered in the lecture auditorium. One case after another, the staff rattled off the achievements of the children in our group. We all clapped for each child, and the milestones they had achieved. I was so happy that so many had climbed up the ladder of brain healing and growth. I wondered what they would say about Carla. Perhaps they would be impressed with the expansion of her chest cavity, or her pupilary responses or the improvements in her crawling ability. I was nervous and eager to hear her name spoken.

Just as soon as they began, they were finished and got up to leave the room. What was happening? I couldn't believe it. They hadn't said a thing about Carla. I looked around and noticed there were several other parents whose children had not been mentioned. It was not easy to sit there and contain myself when I wanted to stand up and scream. What about my daughter? What about the other kids? Why are you not acknowledging us? What about us? Don't we count? The cruelty of it stung. We had not improved significantly enough in their eyes, so we were nothing to speak of. And that is when my bubble burst. The illusion of the Academy as a wonderful salvation was forever destroyed.

After the lecture, I stood outside, speaking with another mom, trying to put what had happened out of my mind. She was telling me how impossible it was for her to do the program and take care of her other two kids. I could sympathize. Doing the program was full-time work. Then she mentioned that she had called the Academy and told them, "I cannot do this anymore. It is just too much. As well as my son is doing, I just can't continue."

Their immediate response was, "Oh no, don't do that. We will work with you. We can change the program around so it will not be so difficult. Your child is making terrific progress and we want to work with you." That seemed so out of character for them, so different from the conversations I had experienced. Then a thought struck at me like a rock hurled by a schoolyard bully. They felt her child was making great progress, so they did not want her to leave the program. They wanted to keep her by any means, because she would be another winning statistic for them. They could tout it to other academies to indicate the superiority of their program. They wanted winners.

It hurt when I realized all this. It hurt me that my child did not matter to them as much because to them, she was not a winner. That's when I saw what my husband had been complaining about. He didn't want to say too much for fear of upsetting me when he knew how deeply I felt about the place. But he had picked up on the insincerity and the intimidation of parents. It was harsh to awaken to their attitude. I had believed that these people truly cared about all brain-injured kids, not just the achievers. It was a true wake-up call.

I wasn't about to give up though. Although I was no longer starry-eyed about the Academy, I was determined to persevere for Carla. As much as I didn't like some aspects of the way they did business, I knew they still had the best program available for Carla right now.

On the ride back home after our grueling week, I looked down at my hand and noticed something missing. The large opal in the ring my husband had given me last Christmas was gone. I shook my head in disbelief. I was always so careful with that ring because I knew how delicate opal stones are. I couldn't imagine where in the Academy I had banged it against anything hard. The next day we called the Academy to see if anyone had found it. We combed the van from top to bottom looking for it. Nothing. "Oh well," I sighed to myself, "A bad ending to a bad week."

Getting back into our routine of doing the program with Carla was now very much a part of us. There was little variation in our routine. The days I worked, I would come home at seven and relieve Bob. Usually it would be Carla's feeding time, so while I fed her, I would eat some dinner with her. Then we would resume doing program until half past eight. Then it would be bath and snuggle time, and I would prepare her food for the next feeding. At nine thirty I would go to bed. Bob would take over until eleven, when the night nurse would show up.

Many a night I would come home and find Carla and Bob collapsed together sleeping on the sofa, her suction machine at his feet. Anora would warn me, "Shh, Mommy. Daddy and the baby are sleeping." The two of us would have some alone time while they napped. Carla always looked so snug and secure in my husband's arms. Every time I saw them together like this, my heart filled with gratitude. Gratitude for having a husband so devoted to his daughter—as loving to Carla as he was to Anora. Never a complaint from him about how much work Carla was. Never a comparison to our healthy daughter. He loved her just as deeply as I did. I thanked God for giving me the perfect husband, and for giving my children the perfect father.

I also thanked God for giving me the perfect parents, so I could be taught the invaluable lesson of unconditional love. After these many months of taking care of Carla, I realized I was not the same person I used to be. I had been the kind of person who didn't like to be too inconvenienced by anyone or anything. I thought taking care of myself was a top priority. Now I saw clearly how shallow my life had been, how selfish. As tired as I was most of the time, I had something many others did not. I had a huge purpose outside of myself to keep me motivated every day—the well-being of Carla. I realized with gratitude that the seeds of an unconditional willingness to give to another had been planted all my life through the actions of my mother and father. There had been plenty of times during my growing-up years when my mother and father could have given up on me, believing that I would never amount to much. But they didn't. They loved me through every tough time.

I was secure in the love of my family and my devoted friends. It seemed that each time I hit a low point, my friend Carol, my calling angel, would ring me up on the phone. "I just wanted you to know that I am thinking of you and Carla, and you all are in my prayers," she would say in her heartfelt way. It was always so comforting to hear from her—my little pick-me-up for that day.

My friends Michelle and Jan would come over each week and help pattern Carla. Jan lived the closest to me. So often, if we were in a pinch, we would call her at the last moment. Without hesitation, she would round up her three daughters and head on over. Her adoration and love for Carla were strong. She frequently would bring special little healing trinkets to put near Carla's bed. She was also the only one who ever spoke of Carla as well and healed in the future tense: "When Carla graduates from high school…When Carla is ten, won't she just amaze everyone with what she can do?" I was so grateful that someone had such faith in Carla's future. All the love that surrounded me kept me afloat when everything else was always going topsy-turvy and upside-down around me.

Jan's mother, Joy, would occasionally come to visit from New Orleans. During one of her mother's visits, Jan told me that she would really like to meet Carla, as she had heard so much about her. Joy was a special lady. I say lady, because she was your classic southern belle, from her slow, melodic way of speaking to her elegant manner of dress and demeanor, even in her wheelchair. When she spoke, her graceful hands would either fold neatly in her lap or she would use them in exquisitely deliberate gestures to illustrate one of her many wonderful stories.

I thought it would be a great idea to have Joy, her companion, Peg, and Jan over for a lovely little brunch. I like to cook, and I knew they all liked to eat, so we had a leisurely time of dining and companionship around the table. I told them it was now time for Carla to eat, so into the living room we all went. At that point, we had a special new standup device that we would strap Carla into during feeding time. Joy leaned forward and watched in fascination as I put Carla in, and then fixed her food. Afterward, I lay Carla down for a nap as she seemed tired. We were all relaxing in the living room, stealing glimpses at Carla as she napped, when Joy began telling anecdotes of her days as a special education teacher.

When Joy would begin one of her stories, I would just settle back and down in my chair, because I knew I was in for a treat. She was a master storyteller. Apparently, Carla thought so too. Suddenly, out of her nap, she lifted her body up and twisted her little head around, as if to see where this lovely sound was coming from…Joy was just tickled to see her response, and beamed, "Why Carla, do you want to hear the story too?" After that afternoon, Joy was smitten with Carla and counted herself a member of Carla's ever-widening circle of friends.

Chapter 18

Information-Gathering

Another flyer for another seminar. As a chiropractor, I received information on all types of healing seminars almost weekly. This one was all about nutrition and for some reason it piqued my interest. It was always hard to decide whether or not to go to a seminar. To go meant losing time with Carla and having to replace myself for that time period. Would this be one of those times I would actually learn something of value for Carla?

Even the night before the seminar, I still hadn't made up my mind whether or not to go, although I had looked on a map and figured out how to drive the two-hour distance. That Saturday morning when I woke up, however, I knew I should go. I got up early and readied myself for the drive.

I was just about the last person to enter the seminar room. The room was darkened and everyone was watching a movie of sorts of nature stills with dramatic music playing. "Oh no, I said to myself. The hype has begun already." I had been to too many other seminars where the dramatic presentations made up for the inauthentic products being promoted. My fears were intensified when the music stopped and the usual dramatic testimonials proceeded. A young, good-looking male doctor got up and spoke of how his life was just ruined from chronic fatigue syndrome. He could not get out of bed and his practice was failing until he was evaluated by Dr. Adams and started on his recommended program of nutrition.

Following several testimonials, Dr. Adams began his talk. He had that flair of style and speaking, which in my mind, I equated with quackery. He came off like an infomercial salesman. As the morning progressed, however, I realized he had a lot of information that I had never been exposed to. He spoke about the importance of giving the correct nutritional products in the correct sequence, of knowing how to evaluate a person's individual biochemistry. He also explained the damaging effects of accumulated toxins and infections, the symptoms they produced in the body, and the means for getting rid of them.

At break time, many doctors and nutritionists wishing to ask personal questions surrounded him. I was among the group hoping to ask him about Carla. All of a sudden I heard the words, "my brain-injured child" and caught a glimpse of the smallish woman with straight brown hair and large glasses who had uttered them. I made a mental note to find her after I had a chance to speak to the doctor. I never did get a chance to elbow through the crowd around Dr. Adams. But I did see the woman chatting with a vitamin company representative, so I decided to go over and speak to her.

"Excuse me," I said. "I heard you mention something about your brain-injured child. I have a brain-injured child also. Could I speak to you for a minute?"

"Sure," she replied in an upbeat manner. For the next few minutes I felt like I had entered another world, a world where another mother had gone through some of the same hell I had, and had succeeded in making her son well despite all the negative prognoses. This woman, Doctor Hanna, was a naturopathic doctor who had given birth to a brain-injured boy twelve years ago. She had been through similar horror stories. Medical doctors told her not to expect her boy to live. Her son had seizures day and night. She and her husband had to take turns staying up at night with him to make sure he didn't stop breathing. She had been to a world-renowned geneticist who told her that her son had a condition so rare there wasn't even a name for it.

"That," she said, "was my turning point. That is when I knew medical science didn't have a clue, and I was on my own." I listened with fascination. "Today my son is twelve. He has no seizures, and does high school math! He is not walking yet, but I am sure that someday he will," she continued with confidence. "I learned this work, added some of my own knowledge of herbal products, and that's why I am where I am today."

She told me how she learned of herbs first-hand from her European mother who would take her out in the woods and explain what the herbs could be used for. Her background echoed mine. Part of the reason I was so drawn to natural healing methods was because of my own mother. As a child I watched my own mother refuse to have her tonsils removed, and instead, gargled her way back to health. With various health potions of cabbage juice that she would make herself, I saw her heal my father's ulcers. Whenever my brother or I were sick, some sort of healthy concoction would be made for us. Adelle Davis' book would be pulled out for a remedy. I had learned about healing the body naturally in my own home. Dr. Hanna was about to continue with her fascinating story when we were interrupted. It was time to head back to the lecture.

As everyone started to move back into the lecture room, I did not want to move. I just wanted to stay put and find out more from this unpretentious woman whom I felt knew a hell of a lot. She turned out to be sitting right in front of me. I listened more attentively now to what Dr. Adams was talking about: a simple system of testing all the acupuncture points on the body with something called kinesiology or muscle testing for deficiencies, toxicity, infection. Part of me was saying this is a little far out while another part was saying listen and learn.

At the next break Dr. Hanna volunteered to test me. As she was testing me, she mentioned all types of toxicity in my body: metals, chemicals, parasites. She asked me where I had lived, what kind of water I had drunk. Had I ever done any drugs? She told me how brain-injury in a newborn frequently can be the result of undetected toxicity in the mother. When she spoke of the accumulated damage in a woman's body as she gets older, the wheels of my brain started rolling. For the first time, something was making sense of why this had happened to Carla—on the physical level.

I remembered that five years ago Anora was born three weeks early. There was some abnormality with my placenta, whereby she was not getting sufficient nutrition. Anora had been the skinniest baby I had ever seen. Her color also hadn't been that great at birth. After a couple of months, she had plumped up and grown up to be a healthy child, so I just forgot about the whole thing, although I always wondered why I had problems...during my pregnancy I had been so careful to do everything right. Now I understood it wasn't just what I did during my pregnancies, it was what I had done to my body all the years prior. I had smoked cigarettes and done some recreational drugs in college. I had permed and colored my hair for years. I had lived in a heavily polluted city for a year. I started to see the accumulation of all the things I had been exposed to and understood how it had all affected Carla.

The new realizations flashed in my brain as I pieced together all that she was saying with how I had actually been feeling physically over the past several years. It was startling to finally have some answers that I knew in my gut were right on. I also had a strong feeling this woman knew a lot, maybe even more than the doctor who was speaking.

At the next break people were lining up to have Dr. Adams do muscle testing on them. I quickly got in line behind Dr. Hanna. I still had a lot of questions that I was burning to ask her. Now that I had finally found a doctor who knew something about nutrition and brain-injured kids, I did not want her out of my sight. I could feel her trying to politely distance herself from me. I'm sure I was coming off as being very intense. Normally, I would have been mortified and would have left abruptly, but not in this instance. It didn't feel like I had a choice in the matter. I was absolutely compelled to extract from her as much information as possible.

Before the end of the day I had made an appointment with her for myself and Carla. She lived several hours away up in the mountains of New York. Frankly, at that point, I wouldn't have cared where she lived. If she was halfway around the world, I would have gone to her.

On the ride home I was so thankful, that I had been prompted to go to this seminar and thankful that I had found someone whom I was certain could help Carla. The answers were at hand. I felt truly that it was a new beginning.

Chapter 19

Quality Time

Another frantic pounding on my bedroom door in the early morning hour. Mary, the nurse, screamed, "She stopped breathing. I called the rescue squad!"

Carla lay on the floor in her all-too-familiar limp manner. "Carla, baby, don't you die on me," I commanded her. Before I could say or do anything more the rescue squad were right next to me, giving her oxygen. In the next moment Carla was breathing and alive.

"Mary, what happened?" I asked in confusion.

"I don't know," she replied, "She just stopped breathing. I went to the oxygen tank. It was empty, so I called the squad."

The whole scenario made no sense to me. Mary had been with us for a while now and I had come to trust and like her. She had knitted a beautiful baby blanket for Carla. I had been touched when she gave it to us. I knew by the arsenal of coffee she brought with her each evening that I didn't have to worry about her falling asleep on the job. Bob had voiced some initial concerns about her being a smoker. He wondered how could she go eight hours without a cigarette. When she assured us she could go without, I had believed her.

The next morning Bob happened to be looking outside his studio door. His studio was at the end of the house away from our bedroom and the living room. The snow was starting to melt. He looked down and found a pile of cigarette butts. Mary had clearly been sneaking cigarettes outside, and hadn't gotten around to removing all the evidence. Slowly we realized what had happened. She had come back into the living room after a cigarette to find Carla not breathing and she panicked. She couldn't get the oxygen tank to work in her panic and called the squad. We were incredulous at the whole incident. We checked the oxygen tank. It worked fine. We always had a tank of oxygen next to Carla's bed for such incidents, and we always checked its fullness.

It was a huge betrayal for both of us. We were forced to realize that someone we trusted had lied to us for a long time and had put our baby in jeopardy by leaving her alone for cigarette breaks. It was the first time I ever saw Bob so rattled, so completely angry. That weekend, in the midst of a family dinner, he broke into a tirade of what had happened and how he would have sued the nursing agency's ass if anything had happened to Carla. I knew it was just his way of venting his upset. He would never sue anybody. He's just not a vengeful person.

Seeing his upset made me realize something important. My husband and I needed a break away. Through the past year we had consciously been doing little things to take care of ourselves so we wouldn't burn out. Every week I would faithfully deliver myself into the loving hands of my massage therapist to relax in her hands. As often as possible, I would make sure Bob got out to do some golf—his relaxation. But we hadn't done anything together for a long time as a couple.

I had a brilliant idea. I was sure it would get my husband's attention and approval. "Honey, what do you think of just you and me spending the night together away somewhere?" I asked suggestively. "You know, just you and me and a good time?" I enticed, wrapping his arms around me.

"But where would we go?"

"To the one and only hotel in town—the Holiday Inn."

"Sure thing," he replied without a blink, knowing full-well what I had in mind.

We needed a break away from our kids just like any other couple. We had just been too afraid to go anywhere for so long. But we would only be five minutes away, and it would give us what we needed—a sense of normalcy and some fun.

That very weekend we were at the front desk registering ourselves for the night. I have a "thing" about signing in at hotels, I always feel the people behind the desk are wondering, "Is this couple for real, or are they just having a good time together?" Plus, there is quite an age difference between us, and I had been mistaken before for a girlfriend and not the wife. My husband was in his good humor and couldn't pass up on this opportunity to embarrass me.

"Yes. I would like to sign in for the night," he said, "Just ONE night," (winking at the guy behind the desk). "I'd like to sign myself and my girlfriend—Oh. Did I say girlfriend? No, I meant my wife—for the night—and," he paused for effect, "we would like a really BIG bed." I stood next to him feeling the flush starting in my face.

"You just couldn't help it, could you Bob? You had to do it," I thought in my head.

With that over, we proceeded up to our room. As we walked in the room I reminded myself, "You are here to have a good time, to think of nothing else for this one night except you and your husband." And a good time is exactly what we had.

The next morning I had set the alarm for six-thirty. When it rang, we both jumped up and hurriedly got dressed. The get-away was over. We had to be back at the house before seven o'clock when the night nurse left.

When I picked Carla up her little head was oily and she smelled so fragrant. Our new night nurse was an Indian woman, very caring and wonderful with Carla. She also massaged Carla in the traditional way of Indian women. The special oil she used was a delight to the senses. "Oh I am so happy you had your nightly massage sweetie," I said to her. And I am so happy to see you." We had all been pampered and sensually nourished that weekend.

Chapter 20

Christmas Eve Carla Turns Two

Christmas time was drawing near. And just as important it would be Carla's second birthday on December 24. I made a mental note of whom I would invite to her party, what kind of cake I would make, and what pretty dress Carla would wear. Just like any other two-year-old she was going to have a party.

The day of her party she wore a pretty red dress, had two candles on her cake and listened to us sing Happy Birthday. I couldn't believe two years had already gone by. Amongst all her presents was a special gift from Edna. She had framed a poem written just for her.

A Anora is the big sister.
B I am the Baby sister.
C My name is "Can-Do" Carla.
D "D" is for our wonderful, loving Daddy.
E Expect miracles.
F Friends send good vibes.
G God is helping.
H Hallelujah! I'm here.
I I is the me I am becoming.

J Just believe!
K We Know that in all things, God works for good.
L Lucky me, to be so Loved and to have such a
M Wonderful loving Mommy
N "There are No Negatives."
O Oh the songs I've been sung!
P More things are wrought by Prayer than we dream of.
Q At night it is Quiet.
R And I will Rest.
S And dream of Someday.
T Good Thoughts make me strong.
U Upward is the way!
W Weave me the sunshine.
X For I am the X-mas baby.
Y And Yes! Jesus loves me
Z Blow lightly and gently on me, o thou Zephyrs.

In its corner was a picture of Carla. I read it over and over. It was so perfect. It summed up everything we felt about Carla. "So many people love you, Carla. And who loves you most of all?" It was a question to which she had heard the answer many times. "God loves you most of all. That's right. And he will help you get well. We'll just keep on praying baby. We'll just keep on praying."

On Christmas day I had the biggest surprise present of all. In a beautiful velvet jewelry box was a gorgeous opal necklace from my husband. It was an exquisite design. I loved it.

"Does that opal look at all familiar to you hon?" he asked. I looked puzzled. "Several weeks after we had given up finding the stone to your ring, something made me look in the van one more time," he continued, "and what did I find? A big piece of the original stone. So I decided to have a necklace made." I was so thrilled and amazed.

"Thank you God for small miracles. I'll take them!"

Chapter 21

A Mystery for God to Solve

It was January. Time for Bob, Anora and my mom to make their trek to Florida. I made my usual preparations to take time off from work, and Edna agreed without hesitation to come stay with me again. It would be another cozy week, the three of us happy to be together.

"Brr," Edna shivered, coming in from the cold. "It is getting nasty out there."

"Yup," I replied, "We're supposed to get a good snowstorm." I had no fear of snow. My only concern was losing electricity. We were so absolutely dependent on it for Carla's equipment: her pulsoximeter and most importantly, her suction machine. I watched the snowflakes coming down heavier and heavier. The temperature was dropping further and further.

Around ten o'clock it happened. The lights went out. Just as I was about to suction Carla. "Damn," I cursed out loud, "It had to happen at nighttime."

My mind raced to figure out how I would deal with the loss of electricity. Specifically, I had to find a way to suction Carla. I decided I had no choice but to call the rescue squad. "Listen, this is my situation," I told them, "I have no electric. And I have a child who absolutely must be suctioned every couple of hours at the most." They agreed to come over and let me use the equipment they had in their van.

A few minutes later they pulled up outside of my house. I bundled Carla and walked the few steps into the van. "Thanks so much," I said, relieved. "From what I hear, we are going to be without electricity for the rest of the night." They agreed to come several more times during the night.

I moved Carla into Anora's bedroom. It was the smallest and warmest room in our house. I put Carla's food and milk into a container and floated it in our hot tub; that would stay warm for awhile too. Having figured out the best I could do, Edna and I camped out in the bedroom with Carla. "This reminds me of some of my favorite camping stories...." Edna started. I held Carla comfortably in my lap while she entertained us with her girl scout camp experiences.

We were grateful when our night nurse showed up. "What's going on?" she asked. "I figured either you didn't pay your electric bill or you decided to be old-fashioned for a night when I saw your house all dark," she joked.

"Well come on in," I said as I led her to Anora's room. "Come join the party."

The next morning we had a good two feet of snow outside. I looked helplessly at our driveway. It was impassable, and I was not about to shovel it. Outside I heard the unmistakable sound of a snowplow going past our house. Just what I could use. I looked outside. It was going in the wrong direction, down the street towards the highway. "Edna," I yelled, "Watch Carla. I am going to catch that snow plow!" I threw my coat and boots on and ran like a maniac down the street.

Out of breath, I caught up to the man. "Please," I begged. "Can you come and do my driveway?"

"Sure thing lady. No problem."

"You owe me big time for this Bob!" I said in my mind as I trudged back to the house.

The snow stopped our nurse from showing up the next night, so I told Carla, "It's camp-out time for us honey. Me and you on the living room floor. You know I'm not a night person, but tonight I'm your nurse." The first couple of hours went easily. By three o'clock I was getting so weary.

But it was time to feed Carla, so into the kitchen I stumbled to get her food ready.

After her feeding, we both slept for an hour. Then her pulsoximeter went off and I had to suction and reposition her. By 7 A.M. I was praying fervently, "Please God, let the day nurse show up." Like an angel, she did, and I fell into bed, exhausted.

The next night—no nurse again. Carla wasn't having a good night either. I didn't know what was bothering her, and I couldn't get her into a comfortable position. She kept arching and would not fall asleep. I did everything I could think of. I suctioned her, thumped her back, rubbed her back, held her, talked to her. Nothing was making a difference. By now it was past midnight.

I was so tired, my mind snapped. I lost it with Carla. "What the hell is your problem anyway?" I snapped at her angrily. "You don't want to go to sleep. Well then, we'll just do your program—see how much you like that." I grabbed her from off the floor and practically threw her on the incline plane.

In the next second I realized what I was doing. I sensed the fear in Carla with my words and actions. I picked her up, fell down on the floor with her against my chest, and just cried. I cried at my cruel words—for having lost it with a baby like Carla. I cried for the hopelessness of our situation. "Help me God," I pleaded, "Give me the strength I need." That comforting feeling I had so long ago seemed like a vague dream. I was so tired physically, spiritually, emotionally.

The following week everyone came back from Florida. I did a double-take when I saw Anora. She was so brown. Her hair seemed lighter. And she must have grown an inch while she was away. I looked at her and asked my husband, "Are you sure you brought the right kid home from Florida? This one looks different from the one who left."

Anora just laughed and kept telling me, "It's me mom. Really, it's me."

I was so glad she could go away and have undivided attention from my mother, who adored her, and my husband. Not that we ignored her—we made special times for each of us to be with her, and she never complained about all the extra attention Carla received. It felt right that she was learning such valuable lessons at a young age. She was learning what it means to be family, about giving of oneself when needed, of taking care of each other. I could see she was also learning another critical lesson, that sometimes life just isn't fair, but the best can still be made of it. The academy had told us many stories of siblings of brain-injured kids. They intuitively knew more had to be given to the injured child. It was only some of the so-called experts who would bemoan the situation with the idea that these siblings were cheated of a normal childhood. The experts considered it unfair to make anyone's needs secondary. It was also the so-called experts' opinion that children like Carla should be put away in institutions for the sake of the family. It burned me so when I heard such opinions.

I was overreacting a little too much to everything lately, and decided to go away a couple of days by myself. I picked a spa at the end of eastern Long Island. "Carla," I said, "I am going away just for a couple of days, and I will be back in no time at all. I'm going away for some R and R." I booked myself for three long days.

Blissfully alone, I drove the three hours to my spa on the beach. I checked in and was shown my room. It overlooked the water. I would be able to hear the sound of waves crashing all night, one of my favorite soothing sounds. My very own private, quiet room with cable TV and video. Wow! What a treat. It was the middle of winter, so I practically had the place to myself. There was almost no one in the dining room. It was fine with me. I was in no mood to make small talk with anyone. I just wanted to rest, recoup and be pampered.

And pampered I was. The next day I had a massage, a facial, a swim in the pool, an exercise class. In the afternoon I rented a video. I looked at all the titles with confusion. I had no idea what any of them were about. I hadn't been to the movies or watched much TV for two years now. One title caught my eye. I remembered a patient saying she had seen it, and it was hilarious. I went back in my room, flopped on my bed and popped it in. Practically from beginning to end, I laughed. What a delight to be so completely diverted from my life for a few hours.

The next day was a repeat of the first. By now, I was really starting to like this place. After lunch I went for a long walk along the beach. I savored the cold wind, the crunch of my feet in the sand, the smell of the seawater. At night I slept soundly after "talking" to Carla, telling her how much I loved and missed her.

The next morning I awakened uneasily. I was scheduled for one more day, but I knew for whatever reason that I was being called home. I quickly cancelled my appointments and readied myself for my departure. My retreat was over. It was time to get back to Carla.

As soon as I walked in the house I saw the worried look on my husband's face. "She just started spiking a temperature, hon. I'm not sure what's going on." I felt no surprise. I just took her in my arms and held her. With a sinking heart I knew something was seriously wrong again. We set off for the hospital.

The doctor examined Carla. Another case of pneumonia. How could it be? And how many times can she keep having pneumonia? Back upstairs we went. I knew the routine so well by now. It was like a recurring dream.

That night I felt such despair. I called my friend Barbara, whom I had been turning to during every crisis for the past two years. "Barbara," I said, "We're in the hospital again." She listened quietly to my tale of woe.

"I don't know what else to tell you Cindy. I don't have any more answers for you."

"What?" I was stunned. "If you don't have any more answers, then who does?" It was the first time I felt so completely alone. Before, there had always been advice, an upbeat attitude. I realized it's just me now. I am in a place where few have ever been, a place so hopeless, no one knows what to say. Truly, there were no more human answers.

When Carla finally came home I still had such a despairing attitude. I felt beaten. "What is going on God? Am I not doing everything I possibly can? Am I not nurturing Carla on every level—emotionally, physically, spiritually? Haven't I found all the best people to help us? Then why, *why* aren't you healing her? And what were those words I felt anyway when she was born—just a lie?" I couldn't get it. I was upset. My human mind just could not comprehend why Carla was not receiving the blessings that I thought were best for her. Only later would I realize I was dwelling on my own ideas of what was best. But my thoughts were not what God or Carla had in mind at all.

I put on one of my favorite Amy Grant tapes. At the end there was a song about children. Often I would hold Carla while playing it, singing to her as if she understood every word. I felt it was practically written for her. The chorus continued: "For every single little boy and girl, heaven plants a special seed...red and yellow, black and white. They are precious in the Father's sight..." The words always went straight to my heart. They expressed something I felt deeply. When the tape was finished, I put Carla down for a minute to rewind it.

As I started to put the tape in its cover, I felt the most peculiar sensation. The sensation was coming clearly from Carla. I turned so slowly to look at her. As I did, she looked at me so directly and so intently, I could barely breathe. For a moment, time was stilled. Her blue eyes penetrated through me to a place I did not know existed. It was a look conveying something significant, but I did not know what. It wasn't the look of a baby. It was the look of pure love and understanding. It filled me.

And it was over. She turned her head off to the side in her usual twisted position. I still could not move. What had transpired was so profound I could not speak. I could not comprehend. I could only wonder...such a precious moment, so dear. And what was it she was trying to convey? I truly had not a clue.

Chapter 22

Release

Carla was having what I called one of her goopy days when her secretions were a little more than normal. She was not her usual perky self. "I know you have some catch-up work to do at the office," my husband commented. "Why don't you take Anora to the office with you for a bit? I'll stay here with Carla. We'll both just rest together."

"Okay," I said. "I have some filing work in the basement that I'm sure Anora could help me with."

It was always fun for Anora to come to the office. She liked sitting at the front desk drawing pictures for me and poking around in the drawers. After a few minutes we went to the basement. While we were down there I heard my answering machine ring, but figured I'd be back up in a minute. I'd just get it then. As soon as we were finished, we headed upstairs, ready to head home. "Oh, the answering machine!" I remembered. "Let me get it quick."

My husband's voice was waiting for me. "There has been an emergency with Carla. Come home quick. The rescue squad is here. She stopped breathing."

"Anora!" I screamed. "Get in the car fast. It's Carla!" We ran into the van, slammed the doors and raced the twenty minutes to home. It was a Saturday, and there were too many cars on the road. I sped, weaving in and around cars dangerously.

"Mommy, mommy. You're going too fast. I'm scared," cried Anora in fear.

"I can't help it honey. We have to get home. Carla is in big trouble." I knew that if my husband called the squad, it was not good.

I pulled in the driveway. Bob was waiting for me there, an anguished look on his face. "We'll all go over together. The squad just left a few minutes ago for the hospital." On the way over he told me how Carla had been right next to him in her usual prone position on her pillow. He had become engrossed in a golf game for a few minutes. The next minute he looked over and she was suffocating in the pillow. I knew the scenario. It had happened how many times already?

This time in the ER, they did not have good news for us. "We've just gotten the results of her blood gases, Mr. and Mrs. Snyder, and they are not good. We are having difficulty stabilizing her. You need to understand she is in a critical situation this time."

"What do you mean?" I asked, "Is she going to die?"

"You and your husband have some decisions to make," the doctor began, "Whether you want us to continue to do whatever we can with her in her unconscious condition, or let her die."

Die. Die. That word was all I could hear. Frantic, all I could think to do was call my minister. "If she is going to die I have to have clergy here." In no time he had joined us in the small room where they recommended that we sit and make our decision.

"It looks like you have some serious decisions to make," my minister started solemnly, "of what to do about Carla." The immensity of the situation was too much, my husband couldn't take it. He broke down.

"It's all my fault, this should never have happened." He started to cry. I couldn't bear to see my husband in such agony. I dropped down to his feet, threw my arms around his legs and demanded, "Stop Bob. Don't you dare blame yourself. Stop it!" It devastated me to see my husband blaming himself. I knew it was a freak thing that just happened.

It was too intimate a scene for my minister. He got up and bolted out the door. It was truly a moment for a husband and wife to share. This was definitely a decision my husband and I would make by ourselves. I was very clear how I felt. "I can't do it Bob. I can't let our baby die. I want them to do everything possible to save her."

He looked at me. I knew he felt the same way before he said the words, "I don't want her to die either."

It could not have been more than ten seconds after we had reached our unanimous decision that the doctor walked back in the room with a different look on his face. "I have to give you an update," he said. "The last batch of blood gases shows improvement even though she still isn't conscious. What do you want to do?"

I looked him full in the eyes. "We want to do everything possible to continue the life of our daughter."

After our decision was made, they called Jefferson Wood Hospital to transport her there again. The doctors seemed relieved. They had something constructive to do now. They seemed supportive of our decision.

At Jefferson Wood, I stood outside the pediatric intensive care unit, waiting to be reunited with Carla. I thought of the many times I stood outside the door of an intensive care unit. This time I wanted as much as always to be with Carla, but somehow, I didn't have that same hopeful feeling.

A young social worker came up to stand next to me. I thought she was coming over to share words of consolation, words of sympathy at what had happened. I did not expect a verbal bomb to be thrown at me. "Mrs. Snyder, I am so sorry to hear about what happened to Carla," she started. I nodded, acknowledging her, even as I took note of the tone of voice that was being used. Where had I heard that same sweet condescending tone before? Then she lowered her voice. "I can imagine you must be so upset with your husband at his having done this, do you want to talk about it?"

I could feel my heart sink at the same time as I felt incredible disbelieving anger rise from deep within me. I could not conceive how anyone could be so ignorant—so absurdly tactless. "If you think for one moment that I blame my husband for what happened, you obviously have no idea who my husband is and what kind of relationship I have with him," I replied, emphasizing each word with strength.

"I love my husband," I continued in my mind. "If you could spend one day in my house and see all the love and attention and devotion this man has for this child you would never speak these words to me. If you only knew how devastated he is right now. And if you knew how many times this sort of thing has happened to almost everyone who has ever taken care of Carla you would shut your mouth."

She looked surprised, seemed about to continue, but from the tone of my voice she very clearly understood I wanted no further words with her. Maybe she went and wrote in her book, "Mom in denial again. This time about father." I hoped I would never have to have another conversation with another idiotic social worker.

This time, in the ICU there was the familiar scene of Carla intubated, hooked up to IVs. What was different was that she still had not regained consciousness. She was in a coma. There was also something else markedly different—the tone of the staff towards her and us. I could sense they really did not want us there. It felt like we were some sort of imposition on them. Later I would find out the struggle our doctors had to get them to take Carla one more time. They seemed annoyed that she was here—at the futility of prolonging her life.

I called all the people I thought could help. I called Dr. Hanna first. She was shocked and saddened. She listened as only a mother could to my fears of losing Carla this time. She said she would mail some special supplements to be given to Carla around the clock to help her brain. As soon as the supplements arrived, we made elaborate charts of who would give them and how.

Next on my list was the Academy. I remembered so clearly one of the lectures they had given about coma victims. They had devised a particular program for coma arousal, which they claimed was successful. I was in for another rude shock with the Academy. The first person I spoke to was the medical doctor on staff. I explained the situation to her and asked, "What can we do to help bring Carla out of this coma?"

There was a moment of silence at the other end of the phone. When she did speak, I could barely comprehend that this was the same person who had been so kind and friendly to us at the Academy. "We really can't interfere and tell you what to do when she is in a hospital under the supervision of other doctors," she replied in an aloof tone of voice.

"What?" My mind was not understanding this conversation. They were the ones who had the answers to coma. I remembered that day and that lecture so well. "No, I know you can't give medical orders, but just tell me what I can do to help her now, what kind of stimulation should I be providing?" Another evasive answer from her end. I realized it was futile. She was not interested in helping. I hung up in dismay and took a deep breath. Another hard realization. In their eyes, Carla had now failed—big time. She had failed so badly they wouldn't even give me advice on the phone. No hope, nothing.

I called Dr. Hanna back. She suggested a few things: to put strong smells under her nose, to continue the sensory things we were doing at home with hard and soft material against her skin, to continue to talk to her and talk loudly at times.

Edna, Bob, and I maintained our vigil with Carla, almost constantly at her side. Regardless of everyone else's attitudes, we were rallying around Carla. We were not going to give up on her. I would stay with Carla all day, talking to her and holding her as much as possible. At night, Edna would come to relieve me. I would sleep in the waiting room next to the intensive care unit. It had chairs that could be pulled out. It was convenient because it was right next to the ICU. The only problem was that it had a TV, and invariably, an upset parent whose kid had just been admitted would come in and put it on at full volume. I could understand that watching TV was a way of coping for some parents, but I couldn't take the noise. I searched around the hospital wing hoping for a quieter place I could camp out in. Around the bend by an elevator, I found another waiting room. I noticed there seemed to be no one in it during the day. I would take my chances at night. And miracle of miracles—it had no TV. That night I slept, alone and uninterrupted.

For four days now, Carla was the same. This morning my husband and I were at Carla's bedside as usual. One of the nurses came over to us. "Mr. and Mrs. Snyder, the doctor would like to talk to you...right down the hall. I'll show you the way." We were ushered into a tiny room where the doctor sat at a desk, and next to him was one of Carla's nurses.

I thought to myself, they want to prepare us for the worst again, especially since she is not coming out of the coma. That was also a huge concern for me. Even though she was doing better with her breathing as she always did, she just was not coming to consciousness. Every day her eyes were closed, I would occasionally open them and say, "Carla I know you're in there baby. We're waiting for you to wake up and we'll wait right by your side until you do."

"You are aware your daughter is in a coma that she will not come out of," the doctor started. "Carla's condition is very serious. And we," nodding to the nurse, "want you to know we are very aware of this situation and want to offer you some options." I sat there waiting for the suggestions. "As a parent with a child like Carla, you are allowed to make some decisions," he went on. "Since she is not going to get better, you could decide to withhold food from her. It would take a few days for her to expire, and we would make her as comfortable as possible."

The nurse leaned forward and added in a kind voice, "We would do everything to make her as comfortable as possible Mrs. Snyder."

For one brief second, my mind said, "Oh. Okay. You want to make her comfortable while stopping her food. That would be the best thing to do at this point." The kindness and sympathy that surrounded their suggestion confused my mind as to exactly what they were suggesting. I thought they are suggesting a humanitarian choice. In the next instant I snapped back to the truth of what they were saying. They were talking about starving my daughter to death little by little! To them she was just a severely brain-injured kid in a coma who was going to die anyway, so why not make it now? The absolute horror of it shook me. In my panicked heart I knew I had to do whatever was necessary to get Carla out of this hospital as soon as possible. Before any other humane choices were offered.

I looked at my husband. I read from his face that he was not buying into this either. "No," I said rather emphatically. "We do not want to let her starve. But tell me doctor, what has to happen for us to be able to take her home?" I could tell from their fallen faces they thought I was nuts. I could feel their disapproval. I was not doing the medically acceptable thing.

"Well if that is what you want, she will have to have a tracheotomy performed to ensure her breathing." Oh dear God. My heart sank again. Not another operation…another hole in her body.

I agonized over my decision. I knew I had no choice if I wanted to get her home. I wanted to take her home, to those who loved her, to receive care with dignity. We had been here for a week now. I consented. The next morning we walked down to the little waiting area with her. It was excruciating to leave her again. I felt so numb, so sad that Carla was having surgery again. I grieved for the pain she might have. "Baby, baby, I am so sorry. But you know this is the only way to get you home." I kissed her and rubbed my cheek against hers. "You'll make it through this Carla, and we will go home."

"Everything went fine Mrs. Snyder. You can come see her," the doctor said several hours later.

I tried to mentally prepare myself for how she would look. Seeing her with a hole in her neck made me weak. My mind taunted me, "Did you do the right thing?"

We were out of the intensive care unit the next day to a step-down unit. Here Carla had her own room. She was watched over carefully by the nurses and recuperated quickly. That was no surprise. We were taught how to change the trach, how to wrap the strings securely around her neck to keep it in position. The doctor explained that the advantage of the tracheotomy was that if she stopped breathing, the oxygen would be applied directly to the hole and go into her lungs quickly. It still hurt me to see it.

Arrangements were made for her to go home. They suggested an ambulance to take us home. We said, "No. We can handle her. Let us take her by ourselves." They consented. We drove her home in our van as usual. This time we were all quiet. There was no optimism.

At home we decided to do as much of the program as before. We continued patterning her, stroking her with materials, banging blocks and playing musical instruments. But Carla was no longer in the participatory world. She was somewhere in limbo. I would pull up her eyelids and look at her vacant eyes and close her lids back down again. I kept talking to encourage her. "You're going to come out of this Carla. You're going to make it through this. It's just a temporary setback." I wasn't about to give up on our pep talks. But now I spent more time just holding her. I'd play our favorite Amy Grant songs and just hold her close.

After several weeks we started noticing changes in her body. It was getting stiffer. Sometimes we would stop in the middle of a pattern. She seemed so stiff that we could break her if we continued. She was still breathing fine, but her body was becoming less and less responsive. I wondered where my Carla was. No matter where she was I still loved her and would not give up.

Wednesday morning I got up as usual and got ready for work. I hugged Carla goodbye and told her I loved her. All day at work I felt so strange, groggy—like I was in a stupor. I shrugged it off. That evening as I neared the U-turn to get around to my street, I noticed an ambulance going in the opposite direction towards my house. I thought nothing of it. As I pulled into my driveway I saw the ambulance parked outside my front door. I raced inside to a blur of activity. They were giving Carla CPR. I watched them press their fingers against her chest. My husband was speaking. "She just stopped breathing. I couldn't get her going again. I called the squad. Now her heart stopped." I made as if to go over and help with the CPR but just stood back. A quiet was coming over me, acceptance unfolded its arms. My usual take-control, "think positive" self was being replaced with a blank numbness as my body prepared itself for what was to come.

I took the short ride to the hospital in the back of the ambulance. From the front the young man kept looking back at me with words of encouragement. "We're doing everything we can for her Mrs. Snyder. We'll keep trying." There was nothing I could say in reply. I could only appreciate how kind he was being. He wanted me to know they were doing everything possible.

In the emergency room there was a chaotic scene. Doctors and interns rushed around trying to bring Carla back. Ironically, the pediatrician on call that night was the same man on call the night Carla had first been transported to the hospital.

I sat and watched in a daze as someone tried to take blood out of her thigh. The doctor was applying electric paddles to get her heart going. It was all happening right next to me, yet I felt like I was someplace so far away. I could see her body lying flat, half-stripped, so still. The doctor turned to me. "I've been applying high amounts of electricity to her heart and she is still not responding. Do you want me to continue Mrs. Snyder?"

He wasn't asking me, he was imploring me. Two years ago, I had ascribed only cold impersonality to this same doctor. Now his humanity was in full view. I saw how hard this was for him too. I felt compassion for his sincere efforts well up in me. "Stop," I said. "Leave her alone." As soon as I finished those words the flurry of activity ceased. They all respectfully walked away. I walked over to her. Carla, honey, it's your time now. It's your time now to leave this body. Go home to God. Fly with the angels."

I realized those words of so long ago were finally coming true. They were not being fulfilled in the way a mother wanted them to be fulfilled for her child, but the way God chose to provide the best for Carla. She had suffered a long time. Everything was going to be alright. Carla was going back to be with her Heavenly Father, the place she rightfully belonged.

Epilogue
The Beginning—Memories

This epilogue was written by Carla's great aunt, Edna Doll

At the funeral parlor I was waiting for Anora. When she walked in the door she came immediately over to me. I had an assortment of stuffed animals in my bag: a fluffy yellow chicken, a soft pink bunny, and a snuggly little teddy bear. "Which of these do you think Carla would like?" I asked her.

Carefully, Anora picked up each one, made some kind of silent evaluation and said without hesitation, "This one," holding up the teddy bear.

"Shall we give it to her now?" I asked.

"Yes" said Anora confidently.

We walked through the crowd of people and up to the coffin where Carla lay in her lovely dark green dress, looking comfortable and serene as if she were already in Heaven. Anora lifted Carla's arm, put the teddy bear close to her body, and replaced Carla's arm. She looked at Carla for a moment longer. Not quite content, she lifted Carla's arm again, and this time placed her little hand securely around the bear.

With that job done to her liking, she turned and left, completely satisfied that she had done her last act of sisterly love.

About the Author

Cynthia Snyder is married to Robert Snyder and lives in Annandale, NJ with their daughter, Anora.

Precious in Her Father's Eyes is Dr. Snyder's inspiring true-life account of loving and caring for her profoundly brain-injured daughter, Carla, during the two treasured years of her life.

Support Resources

Author's Advocacy Group

Every Life Matters 6 Dogwood Drive, Annandale, NJ 08801
tel: (908) 735-4914
website: http://www.everylifematters.org
mail: csnyder002@sprintmail.com

Relationships/personal/spiritual growth

The Alivening Project P.O. Box 1368, Land O'Lakes, FL 34639
tel: 813-996-3659
website: http://www.alivening.com email: alive2@gte.net

Disability Resources

Disability Resources c/o Avery Klauber, 4 Gatter Ln., Centereach, NY 11720-1032
tel: 516-585-0290
website: http://www.disabilityresources.org

National Information Center for Children and Youth with Disabilities
P.O. Box 1492, Washington, D.C. 30013-1492
tel: 202-884-8200
website: http://nichcy.org

Bereavement Resources

The Compassionate Friends PO Box 3696, Oak Boro, IL 60522-3696
Tel: 630-990-0010
website: http://www.compassionatefriends.org

Share-Pregnancy and Infant Loss Support
St. Joseph's Hospital, 300 1st Capitol Dr., St. Charles, MO 63301
tel: 314-947-6164
website: http://nationalshareoffice.com

Problem/High Risk Pregnancies

Heartbeat International 665 E. Dublin-Granville Rd, Ste 440, Columbus, OH 43229
tel: 614-885-7577
website: http://www.heartbeatinternational.org

Disability Treatment Centers

The Institutes for the Achievement of Human Potential
8801 Stenton Ave., Philadelphia, PA 19038
tel: 215-233-2050
Written by the founder, Glenn Doman: *What to Do About Your Brain-Injured Child*

Move International 1300 17th St., City Centre, Bakersfield, CA 93301-4533
tel: 800-397-4533
website: http://www.kern.org.edserv./move/

Parenting Support

Parents Helping Parents 3041 Olcott St., Santa Clara, CA 95054-3222
tel: 408-727-5775
website: http://www.php.com

Power of Positive Parenting
Barbara J. Smyly, Director, PO Box 1368, Land O'Lakes, FL 34639-4236
tel: 803-996-3659
website: http://www.alivening.com email: alive2@gte.net

9 780595 127634